KT-563-719

Contents

Introduction

Much Ado About Nothing. Deceptively throwaway words to describe a play that at times comes close to tragedy. The title however has a double meaning. 'Nothing' in Shakespeare's time was pronounced 'no thing' and would sound very like 'noting' (meaning 'watching', 'observing'). *Much Ado About Nothing* (or *Noting*) therefore promises what seems like a contradiction: something frivolously light-hearted which is yet disturbingly serious.

The play is admired for the wit and elegance of its characters, especially Beatrice and Benedick, the warring couple comically tricked into falling in love. Equally popular is Dogberry, the Constable of the Watch, incompetent guardian of law and order in the city of Messina, yet virtually its sole defender against criminal trickery.

Tricks of all kinds fill the play: deceptions, disguises, secrets, eavesdroppings and misunderstandings. Many are light-hearted and frivolous, but some are painfully disturbing, and the play's mood swings from light comedy to dark, life-endangering menace. The source of much of this darkness lies in the divisions and tensions so evident in the play, particularly the struggles, sometimes subtle, sometimes cruel, of personal relationships. The young couple, Hero and Claudio, have their hopes of love nearly tragically destroyed by the deceitfully villainous Don John.

A particular concern of *Much Ado About Nothing* is the position of young women in a male dominated world, expected to submit to male authority and conduct themselves in a suitably 'virtuous' manner. Male attitudes, too, come under scrutiny, their distorted codes of honour and their distrust and fear of women.

Above all, the play is about the nature of love and the power it has to lead men and women into delusion, constructing a 'reality' that they wish to see rather than what is really there. As a dramatist, Shakespeare understood the power of illusion. The deceptive illusions he presents in this play have much to say about the equally deceptive illusions that people create for themselves in the so-called 'real world'.

This Guide will enable you to form your own response and help you see that although the play is deeply rooted in the life of Elizabethan England, it is still sharply relevant today.

Cambridge Student Guide

Shakespeare

Much Ado About Nothing

Mike Clamp

Series Editor: Rex Gibson

CAMBRIDGE
UNIVERSITY PRESS

PUBLISHED BY THE PRESS SYNDICATE OF THE UNIVERSITY OF CAMBRIDGE
The Pitt Building, Trumpington Street, Cambridge, United Kingdom

CAMBRIDGE UNIVERSITY PRESS
The Edinburgh Building, Cambridge CB2 2RU, UK
40 West 20th Street, New York, NY 10011–4211, USA
477 Williamstown Road, Port Melbourne, VIC 3207, Australia
Ruiz de Alarcón 13, 28014 Madrid, Spain
Dock House, The Waterfront, Cape Town 8001, South Africa

http://www.cambridge.org

First published 2002

Printed in the United Kingdom at the University Press, Cambridge

Typeface 9.5/12pt Scala   *System* QuarkXPress®

A catalogue record for this book is available from the British Library

ISBN 0 521 00824 7 paperback

Cover image: © Getty Images/PhotoDisc

Commentary

Act 1 Scene 1

The Messenger brings Leonato a letter informing him that Don Pedro, prince of Arragon and ruler of Sicily, will shortly return to Messina after his successful military campaign. The governor is thankful to learn from the Messenger that so few men of high rank have been killed in the war and pleased to hear him describe the brave deeds of a young Florentine, Count Claudio:

> He hath borne himself beyond the promise of his age, doing in
> the figure of a lamb the feats of a lion. He hath indeed better
> bettered expectation than you must expect of me to tell you
> how.   *(lines 11–13)*

Two young women, Leonato's daughter Hero and his niece Beatrice, have been silently watching and listening. Perhaps they have a particular interest in one of the young men in the army. Branagh's 1993 film version hinted at Hero's prior interest in Claudio by having her attendant gentlewomen say 'Oooh!' mischievously at the mention of his name. Hero says virtually nothing in this opening scene, but her cousin Beatrice is not so reticent. By the time she has finished with the Messenger he may well be begging for mercy!

Beatrice begins to talk to the Messenger innocently enough, enquiring whether a Signor Mountanto had returned safely from the war. The Messenger is baffled – there is no one of that name in the army to his knowledge. But it quickly becomes apparent that she is referring sarcastically to Signor Benedick of Padua (*mountanto* was the term for an upward sword-thrust in fencing, suggesting a flashy swordsman or 'stuck-up' social climber).

The Messenger loyally attempts to say praiseworthy things about his comrade in arms, Benedick, but each attempt is cleverly twisted by Beatrice into an insult. So, for example, when the Messenger praises Benedick's good service in the wars, she assumes the only service he performed was to eat all the 'musty victual' (stale food). Her remarks are witty and amusing, but they are also sharply critical. The comic abuse she heaps upon the absent Benedick in lines 23–65 is impressive: he is a slow-witted fool, a coward, a glutton, a 'stuffed man' (all show and no substance), a scrounger, an unreliable friend and a disease that sends men insane.

Although Leonato explains to the Messenger that Beatrice and Benedick have had many lively skirmishes of wit in a long-standing 'merry war', for a moment the Messenger almost believes what Beatrice says about Benedick. 'Is't possible?' he wonders, only to realise that she is mocking both Benedick and himself. The confident soldier-gentleman back from the war has been attacked and beaten by a mere woman! Desperately, he offers a truce: 'I will hold friends with you, lady', a surrender which Beatrice teasingly accepts: 'Do, good friend.'

Who seems to be the prime target of Beatrice's belligerence and scorn in this encounter with the Messenger – Benedick, the Messenger, or men in general? Beatrice certainly makes it clear that she could never love Benedick. In line 64, she talks of Claudio catching the 'Benedict' disease and going mad ('Benedict' priests were used to exorcise madmen to rid them of their evil demons), but when Leonato suggests that she 'will never run mad' (i.e. fall in love with Benedick), her reply is very forthright:

No, not till a hot January.   *(line 69)*

But does Beatrice mean what she says, or does the lady 'protest too much'? It is a question which will resonate through the play.

The entrance at this point of Don Pedro and his men is the event that sets the action of the play in motion. In Shakespeare's day this would have been an impressive moment as the magnificently costumed lords were greeted by Leonato and the ladies of the house. Many recent productions have highlighted the excitement in Leonato's household at the arrival of the army. Branagh's film showed picnicking ladies squealing with delight as Don Pedro and his men were seen galloping round the bend of a road in the valley below. The ladies then raced to the house to wash and dress ready for the soldiers' arrival.

Don Pedro greets his host, Leonato, warmly, gracefully acknowledging that entertaining himself and his entourage will be a costly business. Leonato answers with equally elegant politeness. Entertaining Don Pedro is not a trouble, for when trouble departs comfort must take its place, yet when the prince departs only sorrow will remain:

> Never came trouble to my house in the likeness of your grace: for trouble being gone, comfort should remain: but when you depart from me, sorrow abides, and happiness takes his leave.
>
> *(lines 73–5)*

The prince's eye then falls on Hero and he enquires of Leonato if this lady might be his daughter. When Leonato replies jokingly that her mother had assured him he *was* her father, Benedick is quick to take the sexual innuendo further and Leonato happy to go along with it:

BENEDICK Were you in doubt, sir, that you asked her?
LEONATO Signor Benedick, no, for then were you a child.

(lines 79–80)

This interchange is very revealing. Although the Elizabethans were very fond of making jokes about men with unfaithful wives (such men were called cuckolds), their banter often hid a very real unease. For a man of high rank, his wife's chastity before marriage and her faithfulness in marriage were of paramount importance, for fear that she might produce an illegitimate child who could inherit his wealth (see pages 67, 70–1). The prince and his illegitimate brother, Don John, may well laugh very uneasily at this moment, for Shakespeare reveals later in Act 1 (Scene 1, lines 114–15 and Scene 3 lines 15–16) that Don John had recently led a rebellion against Don Pedro. This bastard brother has already proved a serious threat to the inheritance of the legitimate prince of Arragon.

Leonato's reply to Benedick's joke also echoes the double standards of the time. While an heiress lost her inheritance if she was found unchaste, a male heir did not, for it was no crime for a man to womanise. What does Hero think of her father joking about her own mother's virtue? Some productions have shown her distinctly uncomfortable, in others she laughed along with the men.

It may be the men's joking about the age-old male double standard that provokes Beatrice to speak, although there may be other reasons: she is secretly pleased to see Benedick, she wants to settle old scores, he is deliberately ignoring her, he is too much the centre of attention.

Beatrice begins her encounter with Benedick with a barbed remark: 'I wonder that you will still be talking, Signor Benedick, nobody marks you.' Unlike the Messenger, Benedick is a much more formidable opponent and replies with assumed amazement: 'What, my dear Lady Disdain! Are you yet living?' (line 88).

And so begins a new skirmish in the 'merry war'. Each one picks up on the other's words, twists them, then hurls them back: ('Lady Disdain' – 'Disdain should die' – 'Courtesy itself' – 'Courtesy a turn-coat', and so on). Is it light-hearted and affectionate banter? Or is it angry and bitter? Many Beatrices have been playful, but some have delivered their lines with an edge of bitterness as though they harboured a long-standing hurt and resentment. Their encounter becomes more acrimonious as the conversation progresses. When Beatrice says she would want no man to swear he loves her, Benedick fervently hopes she means it because that would ensure some poor man escaped having his face scratched. In one production, Beatrice's riposte earned a loud 'Oooh!' from the onlookers:

> Scratching could not make it worse, and 'twere such a face as
> yours were.   *(lines 101–2)*

Who actually wins this verbal spat? Benedick attempts to have the last word. He first expresses the wish that his horse had the speed and endurance of Beatrice's tongue, then quickly ends the encounter: 'but keep your way a God's name. I have done.' Beatrice, however, is too quick-witted to be beaten like that: 'You always end with a jade's trick: I know you of old', she retorts, picking up on Benedick's horse insult (a 'jade' was a vicious, broken-down old horse).

So is it a win for Benedick, a win for Beatrice, or a score draw? One production attempted to show how evenly matched the two were by having Benedick turn away as Beatrice makes her final gibe, suggesting some bitterness and hurt might lie beneath the wit and mockery. Beatrice's final words ('I know you of old') suggest their past history might not have been entirely happy. Were they once close, possibly in love, but now apart? Or is their apparent hostility a mask to hide a long-felt mutual attraction?

Don Pedro now announces to the whole company that Leonato has invited them all to stay with him for at least a month (so the prince was certainly right when he told Leonato the visit was going to 'cost' him!). Before escorting his guests off, Leonato welcomes Don John to his house. It is easy to imagine a certain unease in Leonato's polite welcome and a veiled menace in Don John's reply:

LEONATO Let me bid you welcome, my lord, being reconciled to the
      prince your brother: I owe you all duty.
DON JOHN I thank you, I am not of many words, but I thank you.
(lines 114–16)

Productions have used this exit to highlight both the Beatrice–Benedick and the Hero–Claudio relationships. One Beatrice jokingly placed an empty glass in Benedick's hand as she went off. Another threw down a glove as if challenging him to a duel and he picked it up as if accepting her challenge. In another production, Claudio crossed to exit with Hero, but was intercepted by Don John who escorted her off, leaving a disappointed Claudio gazing after her.

Benedick and Claudio, friends and comrades in arms, do not leave with the others. Claudio seems to have been deeply and suddenly smitten with love for Leonato's daughter, Hero, and wants Benedick's honest opinion of her qualities. Benedick, as usual playing the part of the cynical 'tyrant' to women, refuses to be serious, making fun of Hero's small stature and dark hair. The more Claudio sings the praises of Hero ('Can the world buy such a jewel?'), the more extreme become Benedick's cynical comments about women and love. Finally, when Claudio admits he actually wants to *marry* Hero, it is all too much for Benedick. Why, he protests, does every man in the world seem to want to risk being made a cuckold?

Is't come to this? In faith, hath not the world one man, but he
will wear his cap with suspicion? Shall I never see a bachelor
of three score again?   *(lines 146–8)*

Benedick's outburst is the second of several joking references to female infidelity in this opening scene. A cuckolded husband was supposed to grow horns on his forehead, visible to everyone but the husband himself – hence the need for a suspicious husband to wear a cap to hide his horns so people would not know his shame.

Shakespeare provides an interesting clue to the two men's relationship in the use of 'you/your' and 'thou/thy/thine' forms. There was a subtle social use of these pronouns/adjectives in his time. When addressing one person, the use of 'you' implied distance, suggesting respect for your superior, or courtesy to your social equal. 'Thou' could imply either closeness/friendship towards an equal or the superiority of one of higher rank over a lower. So far in the play the more formal and respectful 'you' pronoun has been used exclusively (even Beatrice and Benedick use it to talk to each other, for example).

However, in the two friends' conversation, Claudio uses 'thou' to Benedick, while Benedick generally uses 'you'. It may signal Claudio's superior status (he is a count while Benedick is merely a 'signor' or gentleman) or a certain distance on Benedick's part, an unwillingness to become too 'serious'. The only time he uses the less formal 'thou/thy' is when he is obviously genuinely exasperated and disappointed at Claudio's desire to get married:

> Go to, i'faith, and thou wilt needs thrust thy neck into a yoke,
> wear the print of it, and sigh away Sundays.   *(lines 148–9)*

So what does each man really think about love and marriage? Claudio sounds genuinely (if extremely suddenly) in love: 'In mine eye, she is the sweetest lady that ever I looked on.' But is this the infatuation of an adolescent? And how seriously is the audience to believe Benedick's protestations that he will never become involved with any woman? His remark that Beatrice is a far more beautiful woman than Hero, if it weren't for her ferocious temper, suggests his woman-hater image may be partly a facade.

When Don Pedro returns to find out what 'secret' has prevented the two men from joining the rest of the company, Benedick begs the prince to force the secret out of him and 'reluctantly' reveals that Claudio loves Hero. As in the Claudio–Benedick conversation, the use of 'you' – 'thou' when Don Pedro joins them signals subtle shades of social status. Although they are all friends, the prince generally addresses the others using 'thou' (to signify both friendship and superior social status), while the other two use the respectful 'you' to address the prince. It is no wonder then that when Don Pedro addresses Claudio with the more formal 'you', the young man is disconcerted that the prince might be mocking him:

> You speak this to fetch me in, my lord.   *(line 165)*

Still sulking a little at Benedick's mocking betrayal of his confidence, Claudio eventually admits the truth when Don Pedro assures him he is serious:

CLAUDIO That I love her, I feel.
DON PEDRO That she is worthy, I know.   *(lines 169–70)*

Benedick, however, just cannot be serious:

> That I neither feel how she should be loved, nor know how she
> should be worthy, is the opinion that fire cannot melt out of
> me: I will die in it at the stake.   *(lines 171–3)*

Benedick's boast that he will never allow himself to love any woman is received very sceptically by his friends, which provokes him to make ever more extravagant accusations. Since no woman can be trusted to remain faithful, he will never marry – no wearing of the cuckold's horns for him, thank you very much. And when Don Pedro hopes that one day he will see Benedick 'look pale with love', Benedick lays down the challenge: if he ever falls in love, they can either put out his eyes with a ballad-maker's pen and hang him up outside a brothel, or stick him in a wicker basket and shoot arrows at him; and if he ever marries they are welcome to stick bull's horns on his head and paint a sign on him saying '"Here you may see Benedick the married man"' (lines 195–9). Shakespeare, with comedy in mind, is obviously setting Benedick up for a mighty fall – and Don Pedro may even have a plan already in mind when he responds:

> Nay, if Cupid have not spent all his quiver in Venice, thou wilt
> quake for this shortly.   *(lines 201–2)*

Some critics see in Benedick's railings against love and women a genuine bitterness and disappointment, rather than light-hearted banter, suspecting that the gentleman, like the Lady Beatrice, also protests too much.

Once Benedick has been sent off on an errand to Leonato, the atmosphere changes. Claudio tells the prince how he had admired Hero before they went on campaign, but was too preoccupied by the coming battle to think more about it. Now, on his return, he has become aware of how beautiful she is.

The characters have so far spoken an elegant, witty and assured prose, but Shakespeare now has his characters switch to speaking blank (or unrhymed) verse. The pulse of the metre, the onward flow of the run-on lines (*enjambement*), together with the heightened language and imagery, give a particular power and conviction to Claudio's expression of love as he tells how his feelings for Hero have changed from mere liking to 'soft and delicate' thoughts of love:

> O my lord,
> When you went onward on this ended action,
> I looked upon her with a soldier's eye,
> That liked, but had a rougher task in hand,
> Than to drive liking to the name of love;
> But now I am returned, and that war-thoughts
> Have left their places vacant, in their rooms
> Come thronging soft and delicate desires,
> All prompting me how fair young Hero is,
> Saying I liked her ere I went to wars.   *(lines 222–31)*

However, Claudio's very first words concerning Hero, 'Hath Leonato any son, my lord?', raise questions about the sincerity of his passionate declaration of love. Social expectations, both in the fictional onstage world and in Shakespeare's England, held that marriage for a man of Count Claudio's high rank had to be carefully arranged. For such persons, it was literally a serious *business*, in which a woman's inheritance was of paramount importance (see page 67).

Don Pedro, however, has no reservations about the match and offers to help Claudio by raising the matter with Hero's father. Then the prince has a better idea. At the masked ball that evening, *he* will disguise himself, pretend to be Claudio, woo Hero with passionate words and win her consent to marry him. Why does Claudio not insist on doing his own wooing? Although such proxy wooings were not unknown in Shakespeare's time, it does suggest that Claudio, the 'lion' in battle, is very much a 'lamb' in love. The scene ends with the two men leaving to get the 'love campaign' organised.

Act 1 Scenes 2 and 3

It is later the same day. Leonato, busy with the preparations for the banquet and masked ball that evening, is interrupted by his elderly brother, Antonio. One of Antonio's servants has overheard Don Pedro confess to Claudio that he loved Hero, intended to tell her of his love at the ball, then, if she agreed, to discuss marriage terms with Leonato. In this world of arranged marriages, Leonato's reaction seems typical. He decides to tell Hero of the prince's possible marriage proposal 'that she may be the better prepared for an answer' (lines 17–18). Marriage to the prince would be an admirable match and Leonato assumes Hero's answer will be yes – whether she loves him or not is immaterial.

This episode is the first of many examples in the play of eavesdropping and 'mistaking' (misunderstanding), because Antonio's servant has of course got it all wrong. The audience knows Don Pedro does not intend to propose marriage for himself. The gullible Antonio believes his servant's report, but Leonato is more cautious – he will wait and see. Later in the play, Leonato will be asked to judge the accuracy of far more serious reports concerning his daughter. His judgement then will be far less rational.

Scene 2 ends with great hustle and bustle as Leonato and his household leave to get everything ready for the banquet. Don John and his henchman Conrade enter to begin Scene 3. Don John has chosen not to attend the supper. He is very much the stock villain of the Elizabethan stage (see pages 70, 120, 121): the bastard son or brother, an outsider, stereotypically jealous, scheming and bad-tempered. Yet Shakespeare gives him a certain degree of individuality. He talks obsessively about himself (using 18 'I's between lines 8 and 27), almost delighting in the fact that he is 'a plain-dealing villain':

> I cannot hide what I am: I must be sad when I have cause, and
> smile at no man's jests   *(lines 10–11)*

When Conrade urges him to hide his malice and ill-humour, because his recent rebellion against his brother has left him with few friends, Don John bitterly expresses his alienation from his brother and all those associated with him, using powerful 'restraining' images. He is muzzled like a dog, shackled to a heavy wooden block, caged like a bird. Particularly disturbing is his comment that he 'had rather be a canker in a hedge, than a rose in his [Don Pedro's] grace' (line 20). A 'canker' was a wild rose, but it could also mean a disease and is linked to our modern word 'cancer'. It is as if his malice and hatred is eating away at him like a disease.

Their conversation is interrupted by Don John's other henchman, Borachio, who has interesting news. Like Antonio's servant, Borachio has been eavesdropping on the prince and Claudio's conversation, but, unlike the servant, has not 'mistaken': Don Pedro plans to woo Hero, 'and having obtained her, give her to Count Claudio' (lines 45–6). Don John immediately starts to think of a way to use this information for his own malicious purposes. Revenge on Claudio, who has gained all the credit for his overthrow, would be sweet. So Don John decides to go to the supper after all and see what mischief can be made:

> Let us to the great supper, their cheer is the greater that I am
> subdued. Would the cook were a my mind   (lines 52–3)

If only the cook thought like him – he could poison the lot of them!

Act 1: Critical review

Act I establishes the play's setting. Eminent and powerful men have briefly put aside matters of war and politics to relax in the company of elegant women and turn their thoughts to love. Yet strains and tensions underlie this seemingly confident and relaxed society. This patriarchal world, with its strict codes of honour, places repressive moral restraints on its young women, as Hero's silence, Beatrice's defiance and the men's persistent jokes about cuckolds and faithless wives make abundantly clear.

The main plot's romantic love-match between Claudio and Hero has been set in motion by Don Pedro with his plan to woo Hero in disguise, the first of many deceptions in the play. Don John, however, intends to thwart his brother and Claudio. The personalities of Beatrice and Benedick, key protagonists in the anti-romance sub-plot, have been established, particularly their hostility to each other.

Character groupings are paired in parallel or contrasting ways: two sister-like young women, one silent, the other sparklingly witty; two comrades in war, one young and inexperienced, the other more worldly wise; two estranged brothers, two loving brothers. The power structure within these relationships is clearly important: allegiance to your lord, loyalty to your friend, devotion to your cousin, duty to your father. Women in this male world must either be passively 'feminine', like Hero, or assertively 'masculine', like Beatrice.

Act I also introduces key themes and preoccupations:

- Male honour and female virtue: Claudio's courage has gained him much honour in the recent war, Benedick fears commitment to any woman lest she shame him by her infidelity. Underneath the male joking lies a fear and mistrust of women.
- Truth and illusion: people in Messina love to deceive and pretend, making it difficult to distinguish appearance from reality, pretence from sincerity. Don John's politeness is clearly a mask, but what of Beatrice and Benedick's hostility or Claudio's love for Hero?
- 'Noting' and 'mistaking': in this deceptive world characters constantly observe, react, interact, even eavesdrop. Many will 'mistake' (misinterpret, misunderstand) what they see or hear.

Act 2 Scene 1

Supper is over. Leonato, Antonio, Hero and Beatrice await the arrival of the maskers and the start of the dancing. It is a quiet, intimate moment which gives the audience a brief glimpse into the governor's family relationships.

Beatrice begins by commenting on the sour-faced Don John, then significantly brings Benedick into the conversation. Her ideal man would be somewhere between the two of them: Don John says too little, while Benedick prattles non-stop. Both Leonato and Antonio warn Beatrice about her sharp tongue. It is obvious that she does not conform to their idea of proper womanly behaviour. Leonato's warning is more good-humoured ('shrewd' could mean either sharp-tongued or sharp-witted), but Antonio is much more bluntly disapproving:

LEONATO By my troth, niece, thou wilt never get thee a husband, if
    thou be so shrewd of thy tongue.
ANTONIO In faith, she's too curst.   *(lines 14–16)*

Nothing daunted, Beatrice takes up Antonio's use of the phrase 'too curst' (too ill-natured) and runs with it. If, as the proverb says, God sends a 'curst' cow short horns to limit the damage it can inflict, then, by implication, He will send a 'curst' woman a short-horned (small-penised) husband. But if Antonio says she is 'too curst', then she will be sent no horns (i.e. no husband) at all, which is just fine by her!

The implication in Leonato's banter is the male assumption that Beatrice really ought to behave like a good girl and get herself married, but she proves herself more than a match for him in this battle of attitudes. When she expresses horror at being scratched by a man's beard, Leonato suggests she may meet a man who has no beard – but she mocks that idea too. Playing with phrases like 'more than' and 'less than', she ingeniously explains how a man with no beard is also useless. Such a man would be no better than a girl.

Beatrice's conversation with her two uncles is laced with sexual innuendo. She suggests, for example, that her ideal man would need a 'good foot' (which could mean penis). She speaks of 'short horns' (small penises) and jokes about cuckold's horns, even suggesting that the devil's horns were a result of his wife's infidelity. Old Antonio sees it is useless trying to teach Beatrice how to behave properly, so turns to lecture his other niece, Hero:

Well, niece, I trust you will be ruled by your father.   *(line 38)*

Hero's future happiness is a more serious matter, so now Beatrice uses her wit to support her cousin and friend. She both acknowledges and mocks the reality of arranged marriages – Hero *will* have to obey her father (in Elizabethan times a father had the legal right to dispose of his daughters as he wished), but if the husband Leonato chooses for Hero is not to her liking, then she should reject him:

> Yes faith, it is my cousin's duty to make curtsy, and say, father, as it please you: but yet for all that, cousin, let him be a handsome fellow, or else make another curtsy, and say, father, as it please me.   *(lines 39–41)*

A woman's right to choose whom she marries is what is at stake here and Beatrice will certainly not accept a husband's authority (an Elizabethan wife was legally her husband's property). God fashioned men out of clay and she has no desire to 'make an account of her life to a clod of wayward marl'. Her idea of marriage is a union of equals.

Have her words had any effect on Leonato? It seems not, because his instructions to Hero before the masked dance begins make it abundantly clear that *he* has already decided:

> Daughter, remember what I told you: if the prince do solicit you in that kind, you know your answer.   *(lines 48–9)*

Yet Beatrice continues to battle for her cousin's happiness, telling Hero not to rush her decision. Wooing, wedding and repenting, she says, are like dances. First the wooing dance, all 'hot and hasty', then the wedding dance, 'full of state and ancientry', to be quickly followed by the long dance of repentance that ends only in death. This time Leonato does take note of Beatrice's worldly wisdom:

LEONATO Cousin, you apprehend passing shrewdly.
BEATRICE I have a good eye, uncle, I can see a church by daylight.
     (lines 58–9)

The entrance of maskers to the beat of a drum prevents further conversation between uncle and niece. Masking was a favourite entertainment in great Elizabethan households. A group of masked and costumed male dancers would enter the chamber and take partners from the assembled female guests.

As the couples begin to dance, Shakespeare presents in turn four rather ill-matched couples, where the lady sees through the man's disguise and has fun at his expense. It is almost as if the women are taking advantage of the masking to redress the balance of male–female power, if only for a moment. Hero, Margaret and Ursula tease or mock their partners; then it is the turn of Beatrice and Benedick:

BEATRICE Will you not tell me who told you so?
BENEDICK No, you shall pardon me.
BEATRICE Nor will you not tell me who you are?
BENEDICK Not now.
BEATRICE That I was disdainful, and that I had my good wit out of
     The Hundred Merry Tales: well, this was Signor Benedick that
     said so.
BENEDICK What's he?
BEATRICE I am sure you know him well enough.
BENEDICK Not I, believe me.
BEATRICE Did he never make you laugh?
BENEDICK I pray you, what is he?   *(lines 92–102)*

If Benedick pretended not to know the man to learn what Beatrice really thinks of him, he pays dearly for his vanity, for his disguise, now penetrated, proves his downfall. He hears himself called a dull fool and a poor liar (some truth in this!) who makes witty comments that are nothing more than outrageous slanders. Men either laugh at him or find his words so offensive they beat him up. The last straw comes when Beatrice says how all the disparaging comments Benedick makes about *her* are neither funny nor hurtful:

BENEDICK When I know the gentleman, I'll tell him what you say.
BEATRICE Do, do, he'll but break a comparison or two on me, which
     peradventure (not marked, or not laughed at) strikes him into
     melancholy, and then there's a partridge wing saved, for the
     fool will eat no supper that night.   *(lines 108–12)*

Some productions have had Beatrice assert her superiority over Benedick in this exchange by pursuing him about the stage. Others have highlighted the ill-feeling between the two by making Beatrice refuse to dance with him – one Benedick was reduced to grabbing a small child for a partner.

As the dancing proceeds, Don Pedro continues his wooing of Hero, a fact no doubt 'noted' by many of those present, then leads Leonato away to speak with him. Hero leaves and the ladies follow her, until only Claudio, Don John and Borachio remain. Don John recognises Claudio despite his mask and sees his chance to do mischief. He pretends to mistake Claudio for Benedick, an 'error' that Claudio is happy to play along with. With pretended concern for his brother's reputation, Don John asks 'Benedick' to dissuade his brother from marrying someone so far below him in rank as Hero. Their mischief done, Don John and Borachio leave Claudio alone with his misery.

Claudio is convinced that he has been told the truth and gives expression to the pain of lost love and betrayal in emotional blank verse. Even faithful friends cannot be trusted in matters of love. If the audience is tempted to sympathise with Claudio, they should remember that Claudio has not yet spoken a single word to Hero. His dramatic flourish: 'farewell therefore, Hero' is surely somewhat premature, for he has never really met her!

When Benedick returns to fetch his friend, he guesses the reason for Claudio's unhappiness, because he too has 'noted' the prince's wooing of Hero. He tries to tease Claudio out of his misery, saying that he will either have to suffer in silence, or be a man and challenge Don Pedro to a duel. Claudio's response to Benedick's taunts: 'I wish him joy of her' suggests he is not likely to fight for his love and, unable to bear Benedick's teasing, he leaves. Benedick feels a momentary sympathy for the 'poor hurt fowl' but has his own wounds to deal with, for Beatrice's mockery during the dance has struck home:

> . . . but that my Lady Beatrice should know me, and not know
> me: the prince's fool!   *(lines 154–5)*

It seems Beatrice has hit upon Benedick's deepest anxiety: do people genuinely find him amusing or do they secretly despise him, as she claims? (Elizabethan aristocrats were notoriously touchy about personal honour and reputation.) Benedick responds to adversity in a very different way to Claudio. Where Claudio speaks his thoughts in emotional, self-pitying verse, Benedick uses more considered and reasoned prose to think the situation through:

> . . . the prince's fool! Hah, it may be I go under that title
> because I am merry: yea but so I am apt to do myself wrong: I
> am not so reputed, it is the base (though bitter) disposition of
> Beatrice, that puts the world into her person, and so gives me
> out: well, I'll be revenged as I may.   *(lines 155–9)*

When Don Pedro enters, looking for Claudio, Benedick is faced with a tricky problem: how do you criticise your prince for stealing another man's woman? He deals with it in characteristic fashion, softening his accusation with humour. Claudio, he says, is like

> a schoolboy, who being overjoyed with finding a bird's nest,
> shows it his companion, and he steals it   *(lines 168–9)*

The prince explains what really was going on, much to Benedick's relief, then mentions that Beatrice had told him that Benedick had been spreading malicious slanders about her. This is too much for Benedick. He explodes, launching into a list of all the abusive things she has said about him! She hurled so many insults at him, he says,

> that I stood like a man at a mark, with a whole army shooting
> at me: she speaks poniards [daggers], and every word stabs
>   *(lines 186–7)*

Benedick's wit is as inventive as ever, but now it is much more personal, focusing on how appalling this fearsome woman is. If Beatrice's breath were as powerful as her tongue, she would infect everything to the far end of the universe ('to the north star'); she could have enslaved and emasculated even the mighty Hercules; she is Ate (the goddess of discord) in fine clothes, risen up from hell; indeed, he heartily wishes someone would conjure her back down into hell, because while she is on earth men are deliberately sinning to get sent to hell for a bit of peace and quiet!

This increasingly acrimonious 'merry war' now reaches a painful climax, as Claudio, Beatrice, Leonato and Hero approach. Actors have sought to mark the significance of the mutual hurt the two are inflicting in different ways. One production had Beatrice listen unobserved by Benedick, while he listed all the tasks he would rather do than 'hold three words conference with this Harpy'. Then he noticed her presence and addressed to her face the words which brought her to the brink of tears:

> Oh God, sir, here's a dish I love not, I cannot endure my Lady
> Tongue. *(lines 207–8)*

For Beatrice also has been truly hurt. Her reply to Don Pedro's remark that she has 'lost the heart of Signor Benedick' hints at a past relationship with Benedick that had hurt her deeply:

> Indeed, my lord, he lent it me a while, and I gave him use for
> it, a double heart for his single one: marry once before he won
> it of me, with false dice, therefore your grace may well say I
> have lost it. *(lines 211–13)*

Although her wit does not falter, Beatrice cannot completely hide her bitterness and disappointment:

DON PEDRO You have put him down, lady, you have put him down.
BEATRICE So I would not he should do me, my lord, lest I should
prove the mother of fools *(lines 214–16)*

'Put down' could also mean 'to lay, have sex with'. Beatrice does not want to get laid by Benedick, for if she got pregnant she would certainly give birth to a fool like him. That 'fool' could also mean 'bastard child' adds to the complexity of her bitter wordplay.

Don Pedro's attention now turns to Claudio. He knows the reason for Claudio's unhappiness but cannot resist a little teasing before revealing that he has kept his word – Hero is to be Claudio's bride. Claudio is struck dumb for a moment and Beatrice has to prompt him to respond. When he finally does speak his first words to Hero he is typically romantic:

> Lady, as you are mine, I am yours: I give away myself for you,
> and dote upon the exchange. *(lines 233–4)*

Hero once again is silent, but she does manage to whisper her love for him in his ear. Some productions have highlighted the charm of this betrothal, but others have taken a more jaundiced view. In the Royal Shakespeare Company's 1976 production, the marriage was clearly an agreement negotiated by the men, Leonato and Don Pedro shaking hands as if finalising a business deal.

Beatrice, however, seems genuinely happy to see her cousin and Claudio betrothed. She pretends to wish that she too were getting married: an independent life is a lonely life. Don Pedro gallantly volunteers to 'get' (obtain) her a husband and Beatrice almost invites the prince to propose, very boldly playing on the other meaning of 'get' (i.e. to beget, or father, a child). It is too long to wait for a son of Don Pedro's (be)getting to grow up, she says, so what about one of his father's 'getting'? Yet, when Don Pedro appears to propose to her ('Will you have me, lady?'), she refuses – a prince is far too expensive a husband for everyday use. Until the late twentieth century, this episode was typically presented as a light-hearted compliment graciously received, but in some recent productions the prince's proposal was seriously intended. Whatever their motives, the prince is clearly charmed by her 'merry heart':

BEATRICE I beseech your grace pardon me, I was born to speak all
   mirth, and no matter.
DON PEDRO Your silence most offends me, and to be merry, best
   becomes you, for out a question, you were born in a merry hour.
BEATRICE No sure, my lord, my mother cried, but then there was a
   star danced, and under that was I born   *(lines 250–5)*

When Beatrice leaves on an errand for Leonato, Don Pedro plans a second piece of matchmaking – between her and Benedick. Claudio wants his marriage to take place almost immediately, but Leonato says that he will need a week to make the arrangements. So the prince suggests that they all have fun over the next few days by tricking Beatrice and Benedick into falling in love with each other, difficult though the task may be ('one of Hercules' labours'). The others agree and follow Don Pedro to hear his plan to out-perform Cupid himself:

  if we can do this, Cupid is no longer an archer, his glory shall
  be ours, for we are the only love-gods   *(lines 290–2)*

Act 2 Scene 2

Don John knows that his attempt to sabotage Claudio and Hero's marriage has failed. Borachio, however, has another plan. He is very friendly with Margaret, Hero's lady-in-waiting, and, at some suitably compromising point during the night before the wedding, he will persuade her to look out of Hero's bedroom window. Don John, not the most quick-witted of villains, fails to see what Borachio intends:

> What life is in that to be the death of this marriage?   *(line 16)*

Borachio explains. Don John must go to the prince and accuse Hero of being a 'contaminated stale' (diseased prostitute). Expressing concern for the prince and Claudio's honour, he should offer to show them Hero in the act of entertaining another man in her bedchamber. Borachio will meanwhile have arranged for Hero to be absent, and he and Margaret will talk together at the chamber window using the names Hero and Claudio.

As in the earlier scene with the three villains (Act 1 Scene 3), the language creates a strong sense of darkness, as if the lights have suddenly dimmed in this happy household. Both men sprinkle their conversation with disease and death images: Don John speaks of being 'sick in displeasure' and Borachio talks of ways to 'poison' the marriage. The 'seeming truth' of Hero's dishonour will force Claudio, Don Pedro, Leonato, Beatrice and Benedick to face the difficult task of distinguishing what *seems* true from what *is* true. If they fail the test, then Borachio is not exaggerating when he claims his plan will be

> Proof enough, to misuse the prince, to vex Claudio, to undo
> Hero, and kill Leonato   *(lines 22–3)*

It is no wonder that Don John promises to pay Borachio a thousand ducats if the plan succeeds.

Act 2 Scene 3

Benedick, unaware of the trick his friends are about to play on him, soliloquises on the foolishness of men in love. Claudio was once a plain-speaking soldier who would walk ten miles to see a good suit of armour, but now he speaks in elaborate flowery language, listens to love songs and thinks only of fashionable new clothes.

There is a smug superiority in Benedick's disapproval of the lovestruck Claudio. He uses rather pompous phrases like 'I do much wonder, that . . .' and 'I have known when . . .' and 'he [Claudio)] was wont to speak plain and to the purpose . . . and now is he turned orthography, his words are a very fantastical banquet, just so many strange dishes'. Although Benedick does not rule out the possibility of one day falling in love, he is convinced he would never behave like an oyster and clam up in a moody silence. So long as love fails to strike him down, he is confident of resisting the charms of any woman:

> one woman is fair, yet I am well: another is wise, yet I am well:
> another virtuous, yet I am well   *(lines 21–2)*

It is clear that Benedick is being set up for a mighty fall when he boasts that only when he meets a woman possessed of every female quality (beautiful, intelligent, virtuous, rich, noble, well-spoken, a good musician) will he be in the slightest bit interested.

Benedick spots Don Pedro, Claudio, Leonato and Balthasar approaching and decides to hide himself in the arbour (eavesdropping, of course, is a favourite pastime in Messina).

The prince and his friends settle themselves, speaking in blank verse as befits the love-obsessed characters they intend to play. Don Pedro asks Balthasar to sing. Balthasar makes a mock show of modest reluctance, but Don Pedro insists. Just at the very moment when Benedick is going to be massively deceived, a blizzard of puns echoes the themes of 'noting' and 'nothing':

DON PEDRO   Nay, pray thee come,
     Or if thou wilt hold longer argument,
     Do it in notes.
BALTHASAR   Note this before my notes,
     There's not a note of mine that's worth the noting.
DON PEDRO Why these are very crotchets that he speaks,
     Note notes forsooth, and nothing.   *(lines 44–9)*

The determinedly unromantic Benedick, however, suspects nothing, merely remarking in blunt matter-of-fact prose on the strange power of sheep's guts (from which lute strings were made) to charm the souls of men.

Balthasar's song comes at one of the turning points in the play, when Benedick learns of Beatrice's 'love' for him. It creates a momentary contemplative mood to allow the audience to reflect on one of the central preoccupations of the play – deception:

> Sigh no more, ladies, sigh no more,
>   Men were deceivers ever,
> One foot in sea, and one on shore,
>   To one thing constant never.   *(lines 53–6)*

If female deception and inconstancy have been the main topics of men's talk, the song reminds the audience that it is the *men* in Messina who are the prime sources of deception and inconstancy: Don Pedro has practised one deception already, is about to start a second and has a third planned; Claudio loved Hero, gave her up to Don Pedro, then accepted her back; Benedick gave his love to Beatrice then took it back; more sinisterly, Don John deceived his brother in war, attempted once to disrupt Claudio's marriage and plans to do so again.

The deception ('gull') which Benedick's friends play on him (lines 81–180) makes marvellous theatre. Benedick should be concealed from his friends, but be in full view of the audience so that his reactions can be seen alongside the conspirators' assumed seriousness, nods, winks, nudges and whispered asides. Although Benedick says he will hide in the arbour, directors have been extremely inventive in finding other suitable hiding places. One production had a cigar-smoking Benedick hide in a tree, periodically peering out through the foliage, sending out puffs of smoke to show anger, amazement and indignation. Another Benedick ran around with a stepladder, climbing it every so often to peer over at his friends. Yet another grabbed a pair of shears and pretended to be a gardener clipping a hedge.

In the late eighteenth and early nineteenth centuries, the gulling sequence was usually played rather soberly by Don Pedro, Claudio and Leonato, with the comedy coming from Benedick's reactions, reflecting Benedick's comment afterwards (line 181) that 'the conference was sadly borne'. Since then, productions have tended to allow the conspirators to play more for comedy. For example, at lines 96–105, one Leonato panicked and dried up at Don Pedro's question

'How, how, I pray you!' forcing the prince to cover up the awkward silence with 'You amaze me', as if Leonato had actually said something. Benedick, however, finds them convincing enough – particularly Leonato:

> I should think this a gull, but that the white-bearded fellow
> speaks it: knavery cannot sure hide himself in such reverence.
> *(lines 106–7)*

Once Benedick has taken the bait, his friends proceed to have fun at his expense, describing his faults and pretending concern that he would mock Beatrice mercilessly if he found out her secret. Don Pedro is particularly enthusiastic in his abuse. Each time the others say something in Benedick's defence, the prince turns it into insult. Hidden Benedicks have expressed their silent anger in various ways: shaking fists, miming threats and insults, brandishing shears.

Confident that their plan has succeeded, the friends go into dinner, leaving Benedick to mull over what he has overheard. Many actors speak this soliloquy directly to the audience as if arguing with a friend and trying to rationalise their sudden volte-face. Some have tried to convey a sense of bewilderment at what was happening to them; others, like Branagh (1993) have reacted with barely concealed delight.

The monosyllabic opening sentence 'This can be no trick' has been delivered in many ways: with hesitant deliberation, smug self-satisfaction, mystified suspicion, horrified surprise. At 'love me?' (line 183) one Benedick's eyes crinkled up in modest pleasure, another flung his arms in the air in ecstasy, while a third spoke as if stunned.

Benedick's decision is instant: Beatrice's love must be 'requited' (returned). Yet for all the audience's amusement at this sudden conversion, there is a maturity and self-critical awareness in his words:

> I hear how I am censured, they say I will bear myself proudly,
> if I perceive the love come from her: they say too, that she will
> rather die than give any sign of affection: I did never think to
> marry, I must not seem proud, happy are they that hear their
> detractions, and can put them to mending   *(lines 184–8)*

He then falls to listing Beatrice's virtues (incidentally, some of the very qualities he listed in his ideal woman at the start of the scene!). She is fair, virtuous and wise – except in loving him – and he will return her love with interest: 'I will be horribly in love with her'.

But realisation dawns on Benedick that he will be the target for a great deal of mockery. He must marshal his defence: a man's tastes can change as he matures, no sensible man would let a few smart-alec remarks stop him from doing what he wants to do, it is his *duty* to marry Beatrice because 'the world must be peopled', a line which often provokes audience laughter, as does his final clinching argument:

> When I said I would die a bachelor, I did not think I should
> live till I were married   *(lines 197–8)*

Shakespeare does not stop the comedy there. Beatrice now appears, sent by Don Pedro to call Benedick into dinner. She no doubt is still smarting from their last encounter at the masked ball. One Beatrice entered carrying a gong, which she periodically hammered while talking to Benedick:

> Against my will (*Bangs gong*) I am sent (*Bangs gong; glowers;
> then very emphatically bangs again*) to bid you (*Bangs gong very
> fast, very loud*) come in to dinner. (*Bangs gong*)   *(line 201)*

She expects mockery and scorn in return, but instead receives ingratiating words and smiles:

> Fair Beatrice, I thank you for your pains.   *(line 202)*

How strange this moment must seem to Beatrice!

At the end of the scene, when Beatrice has departed, Benedick picks over the details of her abuse of him, sees 'a double meaning' in her words and turns them into a message of love. This is self-deception of the most magnificent kind. Yet, if she *does* love him, maybe it is not self-deception at all?

Act 2: Critical review

Leonato and his guests are into the serious business of enjoying themselves: first a 'great supper', then a masked dance followed by a 'banquet'. The festivities cannot however entirely hide the tensions in Leonato's family circle. Leonato and Antonio clearly disapprove of Beatrice's independence of mind and unwillingness to submit to the authority of a husband. They also clearly expect Hero to submit to her father's choice of husband – whether it be Don Pedro or Claudio.

The feud between Beatrice and Benedick reaches its climax at the dance when Beatrice's barbs wound Benedick's pride. The gulf between them is deeper than their witty banter might suggest. Meanwhile, the Hero–Claudio love-match continues to progress, despite Don John's attempt to disrupt the betrothal. Flushed with his success in uniting Hero and Claudio, Don Pedro proposes a second plot to bring about a love-match between Beatrice and Benedick.

The balance and symmetry of the play's structure is again evident. Don Pedro's plot to unite Hero and Claudio is countered by Don John's plots to destroy their union, and the grouping of Don Pedro and his two war comrades is balanced by Don John and his two henchmen.

The play's preoccupation with deception and illusion intensifies. There are playful games of deception with the masked dancing couples, Don John deceives the disguised Claudio, and even Benedick mistakes Don Pedro's intentions. Borachio devises a malicious deceit to dishonour Hero, while Balthasar's song echoes the deception theme at the very moment Benedick is gulled by his friends.

More significantly, the mood of the play has begun to darken. There has been much light-hearted male talk of honour, reputation and virginity. Borachio's plan to slander Hero's sexual purity will bring the play close to tragedy and test the men's moral integrity. Some critics have consequently seen a third meaning to the play's title: 'Much Ado About Virginity', because 'nothing' in Elizabethan slang could mean the female genitalia ('nothing' = no thing). Meanwhile, ironically unaware of the unpleasant plot being hatched against them, Benedick's friends successfully carry out their plot to deceive him into believing Beatrice loves him.

Act 3 Scene 1

It is Beatrice's turn to be deceived. Hero instructs Margaret to find Beatrice and tell her that she and Ursula are gossiping about her in the orchard. Hero then briefs Ursula in the role she must play: when Beatrice comes to listen in on their conversation, Hero will talk of how Benedick is 'sick in love' with Beatrice, while Ursula must take every opportunity to praise Benedick's virtues. Very soon Beatrice enters, trying not to be observed, and the gulling commences.

Beatrice's deception closely parallels Benedick's but the scene has a rather different tone and atmosphere. The men largely spoke in a lively and varied prose, conducive to a more comic interpretation. The women, in contrast, speak entirely in verse, as if love were too serious a matter for riotous comedy, although the plight of the hidden Beatrice has often been played for comedy: one Beatrice hid under a table which she moved around to hear the gossip, while another concealed herself behind a clothes line full of washing. However, in some productions, Beatrice has hidden behind semi-transparent screens or curtains to be seen in frozen silhouette, as if deeply moved by what she hears.

Hero has said virtually nothing in Acts 1 and 2 apart from a brief moment of flirting with Don Pedro (and that probably on her father's orders). She has deferred respectfully to her father, uncle and the prince, been too shy to speak her love out loud to Claudio and never sought to emulate Beatrice's confident chatter. Yet in this scene she takes charge and controls affairs with a confidence that suggests there is more to this quiet, dutiful young woman than meets the eye. There is, for example, the surprising power and conviction with which Hero criticises her cousin, accusing her of being 'too disdainful' and acting like a wild untamed hawk ('haggard'). She woundingly catalogues Beatrice's faults:

> But nature never framed a woman's heart
> Of prouder stuff than that of Beatrice:
> Disdain and scorn ride sparkling in her eyes,
> Misprising what they look on, and her wit
> Values itself so highly, that to her
> All matter else seems weak: she cannot love,
> Nor take no shape nor project of affection,
> She is so self-endeared.   *(lines 49–56)*

Beatrice, in fact, finds fault with every man, whatever his virtue. One critic suggested that Hero is not merely pretending for Beatrice's benefit, but making an implied, unfavourable comparison with her own quiet, reliable, unappreciated, dutiful self. She certainly seems a little overpowered by Beatrice's wit and energy:

> No, not to be so odd, and from all fashions,
> As Beatrice is, cannot be commendable:
> But who dare tell her so? If I should speak,
> She would mock me into air, oh she would laugh me
> Out of myself, press me to death with wit   *(lines 72–6)*

Hero indeed wonders whether it might be more sensible to put Benedick off loving Beatrice. Her words strike a more sombre note for the audience, who are reminded of Don John's plan to ruin Hero's reputation in the eyes of the prince, her future husband and her father:

> I'll devise some honest slanders,
> To stain my cousin with, one doth not know
> How much an ill word may empoison liking   *(lines 84–6)*

All this Beatrice overhears. First she has to endure the shock of discovering that Benedick secretly loves her and then Hero's disparaging comments about her 'carping' nature. When Hero and Ursula leave, Beatrice emerges a changed woman. For the first time in the play she speaks in verse (see page 85), declaring her love for Benedick. Like Benedick, her commitment to return his love is immediate. Unlike him, however, she shows no fear of being ridiculed and embraces her new-found love unreservedly, using for the first time the intimate 'thee/thou'. Although this final soliloquy was often given a comic flavour in the early nineteenth century to parallel Benedick's conversion scene, since Victorian times most Beatrices have made it a revelation of the serious and tender aspects of her character.

Act 3 Scene 2

Benedick was right when he feared he would have 'some odd quirks and remnants of wit broken' on him. As Don Pedro talks to Claudio and Leonato about his plans to return to Arragon when the wedding is over, he says what a pleasure it would be to have the company of

Benedick to cheer him up with his wit and sunny nature, knowing full well that a strangely silent, very miserable Benedick is standing beside him. For Benedick is indeed a changed man: 'Gallants, I am not as I have been.' His excuse? He has 'tooth-ache'!

His friends, however, delight in pointing out all the details of Benedick's sudden transformation: he has shaved off his beard, dressed in extravagant fashion, brushed his hat, washed his face and put on perfume and make-up. All that, coupled with his melancholy spirit, Don Pedro concludes, must mean that he is in love. Recognising that he is beaten, Benedick gathers what little dignity he has left and leaves with Leonato to discuss important private business:

> Yet is this no charm for the tooth-ache: old signor, walk aside with me, I have studied eight or nine wise words to speak to you, which these hobby-horses [buffoons] must not hear.
>
> *(lines 52–4)*

The prince and Claudio, convinced that Benedick wishes to tell Leonato of his love for Beatrice, are delighted to see their plan going so well. Their good humour, however, evaporates almost immediately, for now Don John chooses to make the disturbing claim that Hero has been unfaithful, an allegation that he pledges to prove that very night. He quells their good humour and bluntly makes his allegation:

DON JOHN I came hither to tell you, and circumstances shortened
    (for she has been too long a-talking of), the lady is disloyal.
CLAUDIO Who Hero?
DON JOHN Even she, Leonato's Hero, your Hero, every man's Hero.
CLAUDIO Disloyal?
DON JOHN The word is too good to paint out her wickedness

(lines 75–80)

Claudio and Don Pedro's response is disturbingly quick and savage:

CLAUDIO If I see anything tonight, why I should not marry her
    tomorrow in the congregation, where I should wed, there will I
    shame her.
DON PEDRO And as I wooed for thee to obtain her, I will join with
    thee, to disgrace her. *(lines 91–4)*

It is almost as if the two men have already judged Hero to be guilty. The violence of their response is perhaps triggered by the word 'honour' in Don John's proffered advice: 'it would better fit your honour to change your mind'. The men of Messina may joke of cuckolding, but no honorable man could allow a woman's infidelity to stain his reputation (see page 71). If a modern audience finds such an attitude difficult to tolerate, remember that in some communities of the world today proof of a woman's infidelity is sufficient justification even for killing her. In the previous scene, when Hero said in all innocence, 'How much an ill word may empoison liking', she little knew how savagely her claim was to be proven on herself.

The welling up of male anger is reflected in the disturbing symmetry of the men's speech patterns as the scene ends. Far from 'noting' the truth, Claudio and Don Pedro may well have already decided to 'see' what they want, or fear, to see:

DON PEDRO Oh day untowardly turned!

CLAUDIO Oh mischief strangely thwarting!

DON JOHN Oh plague right well prevented! So will you say, when
you have seen the sequel.   *(lines 97–100)*

Act 3 Scene 3

No sooner has Don John begun to weave his evil plot than Shakespeare introduces the audience to the simple ordinary men whose job it will be to bring the villain and his henchmen to justice. The Watch were the policemen of Elizabethan times, their incompetence a standing joke with Elizabethan playwrights. Shakespeare's watchmen are very English, with English names and attitudes, and spectacularly inept.

Dogberry, the master constable, and his deputy Verges, first select a suitable constable of the Watch and then brief all the watchmen on their night's duties. Dogberry's most outstanding quality is his habit of getting everything backwards. If the Watch are to keep the peace, he says, they must not create a noise by arresting thieves or drunks. People appreciate a quiet night's sleep, so the best thing they can do is have a little snooze themselves – provided no one steals their weapons! As master of the Watch, Dogberry tries to sound impressive and authoritative, but his efforts only result in a confused jumble of words and ideas. His particular talent is for malapropisms (inappropriate, muddled or mistaken use of words, see pages 83–4). George Seacoal, for example, is the most 'senseless' man to be the constable and his job is to 'comprehend all vagrom men' (line 21).

Dogberry was traditionally played as a large fat man full of his own importance and his deputy Verges as small, wizened, but equally incompetent – a double act rather like Laurel and Hardy. The master constable and his watchmen have, however, been portrayed in a variety of entertaining ways: as turbaned Indian soldiers of the British Raj, Italian carabinieri and Keystone Cops.

The strangest and most unnerving watchmen were perhaps in Branagh's 1993 film, where Dogberry became a weird obsessive, but this scene is invariably played for comedy. For example, when in one production Dogberry instructed the Watch to 'call at all the alehouses', they immediately rushed off stage to do just that, and had to be recalled by a blast from Dogberry's whistle so he could complete his sentence. Ironically, for all his incompetence, Dogberry does give the Watch one vital piece of advice (and one final malapropism) before leaving them:

> watch about Signor Leonato's door, for the wedding being
> there tomorrow, there is a great coil tonight: adieu, be vigitant
> I beseech you   (lines 75–7)

As the Watch settle down on the church bench, Borachio and Conrade enter. Thinking they are unobserved, a rather drunk Borachio tells Conrade he has just committed a villainy that will earn him a thousand ducats. Perhaps it is the drink, or a sense of guilt at helping to destroy an innocent woman's reputation and marriage, which prompts Borachio to brood on the rich young aristocrats of Messina and how they mindlessly follow the latest extravagant fashions, mistaking the outer fashion for the inner man. It is as if fashion itself is stealing the truth of who people really are. Twice Borachio says 'seest thou not what a deformed thief this fashion is?' (lines 101–2 and 107).

Conrade, probably also drunk, fails to see the relevance of all this talk of fashion, but Borachio persists. Has his deceitful villainy not just convinced Claudio and Don Pedro that Margaret was Hero entertaining Borachio in her bedchamber? He has overheard Claudio, enraged, vow that

> he would meet her as he was appointed next morning at the
> temple, and there, before the whole congregation shame her,
> with what he saw o'er night, and send her home again without
> a husband   *(lines 130–3)*

Borachio's apparently drunken ramblings have in fact revealed the essential superficiality of much of Messina society's behaviour. Claudio and Don Pedro's response to Hero's 'crime' is swift and shallow. The woman Claudio has so recently sworn to love surely does not deserve such a public humiliation? The cruelty lies in the male code of honour: only a public shaming of the unfaithful woman can remove the public shame she has inflicted on the man.

It is characteristic of the play that this sombre reflection on the falseness of appearances runs parallel with a moment of unbelievably stupid 'noting'. One of the eavesdropping watchmen has completely misunderstood Borachio's every word. When Borachio referred to that 'deformed thief . . . fashion', he was probably referring to the Elizabethan fashions of the day, which involved heavy padding and clothes cut into strange shapes. The Watchman, however, assumes Borachio is referring to a notorious local thief called Deformed and even remembers the man having a fashionably long curl of hair down one side of his head!

Fortunately, the Watch are not so stupid that they do not recognise that some villainy has taken place and promptly arrest Borachio and Conrade. Productions have often turned this into a lively and comic struggle. One Watchman accidentally felled two of his companions before beating Borachio and Conrade into submission.

Act 3 Scene 4

It is a little before five on the morning of the wedding and Hero, with Margaret's help, is getting ready for the ceremony. Hero naturally wishes to look her best on this special day and, as young women have done for centuries, she and Margaret discuss clothes and accessories, deciding which 'rebato' (wired neck ruff) Hero should wear and admiring her 'new tire' (wired headdress decorated with jewels and false curls). Margaret considers Hero's gown far superior even to the Duchess of Milan's new gown.

As they talk of the Duchess's gown, with its hugely expensive materials woven with gold and silver thread, decorated with jewels, its padded 'down sleeves' and 'round underborne' skirts stiffened and shaped with material and more wire supports, the audience cannot help but recall Borachio's comments in the previous scene about that 'deformed thief . . . fashion'. If Hero's appearance is to be similarly 'deformed' by her gown, who will have eyes to see the 'real' Hero? The bride-to-be feels a strange sense of foreboding:

> God give me joy to wear it, for my heart is exceeding heavy.
> *(line 19)*

Margaret seems oblivious of the harm her own indiscreet behaviour with Borachio the previous night might cause her mistress. She jokes about how Hero's 'heavy' heart will 'be heavier soon by the weight of a man', a remark that Hero rather primly finds offensive.

With the entrance of Beatrice, the scene begins to parallel the friends' mockery of Benedick in Act 3 Scene 2, as Hero and Margaret poke gentle fun at Beatrice's literally lovesick appearance. Just as love gave Benedick the toothache, so it has given Beatrice a cold.

Margaret takes the lead in goading Beatrice, hoping perhaps to match Beatrice's wit while Beatrice is temporarily off-form. There is again much potential for comedy in their exchanges (lines 29–70). One Beatrice covered her head with a sheet as she said, 'by my troth I am sick', popped her head out in surprise at Margaret's joke about getting some 'distilled *Carduus benedictus*' for her cold, then covered her head again when Margaret said, 'you may think perchance that I think you are in love'.

Yet for all the comedy, there is a sadness about this small intimate scene with its contrasting pictures of the three women: the heavy-hearted Hero whose wedding day will so soon turn to tragedy, the empty-headed Margaret and the emotionally confused Beatrice who perhaps wishes the wedding preparations were her own.

The poignant moment is interrupted by Ursula, returning with the news that the prince, Count Claudio, Benedick, Don John and all the gentlemen of the town have arrived to escort Hero to the church. The women leave to help Hero get ready.

Act 3 Scene 5

Dogberry and Verges arrive to tell the Governor about the two men they have arrested. Will Leonato discover in time the plot to ruin his daughter? He asks Dogberry and Verges to be brief, ironically unaware of the importance of the news they bring. In one production, Leonato, his mind on the approaching wedding, studied notes for a speech and tinkered nervously on the piano as he listened. Dogberry, a congenital rambler, takes for ever to get to the point, more concerned to put down his partner Verges than to tell Leonato what he needs to know:

> Goodman Verges, sir, speaks a little off the matter, an old man,
> sir, and his wits are not so blunt [he means sharp!], as God
> help I would desire they were, but in faith honest, as the skin
> between his brows. *(lines 8–10)*

The normally polite Leonato becomes exasperated, but the two constables are impervious to insults, and Dogberry mistakes Leonato's criticism that they are 'tedious'. He thinks 'tedious' means 'wealthy' and very generously says that if he were 'as tedious as a king' he would gladly give all his 'tediousness' to Leonato!

Ironically, it is Verges who delivers the news that they have arrested two 'arrant knaves', but Leonato can wait no longer – the wedding is about to start. He instructs Dogberry to conduct the trial himself, inviting the two men to take some wine before they go.

As Dogberry and Verges leave to prepare for the trial, the audience is left in suspense. The villains *have* been caught but there is now no time to prevent Claudio making his public accusation. Will the incompetence of Dogberry and Verges mean the truth will never come to light? Dogberry's final boast that his brain will soon get to the bottom of it all, together with one more parting malapropism, does not inspire confidence:

> We will spare for no wit I warrant you: here's that [*pointing to
> his brain*] shall drive some of them to a noncome, only get the
> learned writer to set down our excommunication, and meet me
> at the gaol. *(lines 49–51)*

Act 3: Critical review

Act 3 seems at first to justify Don Pedro's earlier boast that he could outdo Cupid himself in matters of love. Claudio's marriage is arranged and both Beatrice and Benedick now believe the other loves them passionately. But suddenly events move out of the prince's control. His brother's slanderous allegation against Hero reveals the misogynistic foundations of Messina's male code of honour. Claudio and Don Pedro's anger is swift, their rush to judge Hero savagely premature. Confusion and uncertainty prevail: Claudio doubts Hero's virtue, Beatrice and Benedick's whole world has been turned inside out, and Hero has heavy-hearted forebodings.

As the play moves towards its crisis, Shakespeare alternates the two main plots to create a rapid and confusing alternation of moods. The playful deception of Beatrice and the teasing of Benedick balances the menace of Don John's accusation. The Watch's comic buffoonery contrasts with Borachio's sardonic discourse on the ostentation of Elizabethan aristocrats. Margaret's light-hearted teasing of Beatrice is opposed to Hero's sudden sadness.

To preserve the comic nature of the play, Shakespeare allows the audience to know even before Claudio and Don Pedro's accusation is made that the Watch have, in Borachio, the evidence to exonerate Hero. Tragedy threatens, but will surely be averted.

The contrast between the two love plots is now very clear. The course of Beatrice and Benedick's love has been long and difficult, while Hero and Claudio's 'love' has been as sudden as lightning and built on shallow foundations. Claudio has swiftly fallen in love and secured Hero for his bride. Now, equally swiftly, he plans to reject her. Yet even now they have scarcely spoken a word to each other.

Overhearings, deceptions and misreportings continue. Beatrice is tempted to eavesdrop on Hero and Ursula when Margaret falsely reports that they are gossiping about her. A Watchman overhears Borachio and assumes he is referring to a local con-man called Deformed. Ironically, Don Pedro and Claudio, fresh from their deception of Benedick, are themselves all too easily deceived by Don John. Even more ironically, Beatrice and Benedick begin to discover the truth about themselves through the deceptions of others.

Act 4 Scene 1

The guests assemble for Hero and Claudio's wedding. Productions have often crowded the stage with onlookers, using their reactions to emphasise the public shame and humiliation that Hero and her family are shortly to endure.

Leonato asks Friar Francis to begin the ceremony. Claudio's first response makes it clear that there will be no marriage, but Leonato misunderstands him, thinking that Claudio is making a rather strange play on words:

FRIAR FRANCIS You come hither, my lord, to marry this lady?
CLAUDIO No.
LEONATO To be married to her: friar, you come to marry her.

(lines 3–5)

Claudio, in what seems like a pre-planned parody of the wedding service, begins his denunciation of Hero. He asks her directly if she knows of any impediment to their marriage. Hero says she knows of none. When the Friar asks Claudio if he knows of any impediment and Leonato for a second time presumes to answer for him, Claudio explodes:

FRIAR FRANCIS Know you any, count?
LEONATO I dare make his answer, none.
CLAUDIO Oh what men dare do! What men may do! What men daily
    do, not knowing what they do!   *(lines 12–15)*

The characters have so far spoken in prose, but now Claudio leads the others into speaking blank verse as he wrenches the occasion from celebration to denunciation. First Claudio asks Leonato directly if he freely gives Hero to him. Leonato agrees. Then he asks what gift of equal worth could possibly be given to Leonato in return. The prince (no doubt as planned) answers for Leonato:

Nothing, unless you render her again.   *(line 24)*

This is Claudio's cue to denounce Hero for immorality. He likens her to a 'rotten orange', her outward beauty concealing corruption within:

> Sweet prince, you learn me noble thankfulness:
> There, Leonato, take her back again,
> Give not this rotten orange to your friend,
> She's but the sign and semblance of her honour:
> Behold how like a maid she blushes here!
> Oh what authority and show of truth
> Can cunning sin cover itself withal!   *(lines 25–31)*

It is clear from Claudio's description of Hero that he truly believes he has seen through her deception, yet, ironically, it is he who has been deceived into believing as true what is in truth an illusion.

Leonato assumes Claudio is speaking in this manner because he has 'made defeat of her virginity', but Claudio firmly denies having had sex with her. When Hero asks him if she had ever 'seemed' anything other than chaste to him, her use of the word 'seemed' inflames him even more:

HERO And seemed I ever otherwise to you?
CLAUDIO Out on thee seeming, I will write against it!
> You seem to me as Dian in her orb,
> As chaste as is the bud ere it be blown:
> But you are more intemperate in your blood,
> Than Venus, or those pampered animals,
> That rage in savage sensuality.   *(lines 49–55)*

Some actors have felt uneasy at the harshness of Claudio's language and have tried to soften his rejection of Hero, highlighting his grief and disappointment. Many other productions, however, have fully emphasised his anger (lines 26–55). Some Claudios have physically thrown Hero back at Leonato (line 26) and at least one Claudio slapped Hero's face at line 50. In Branagh's film, Claudio spat at her (at 'Venus', line 54), struggling to restrain his tears.

Leonato turns to the prince for help, but his reply is as brutal as Claudio's. Hero is a prostitute of the lowest kind:

LEONATO Sweet prince, why speak not you?
DON PEDRO   What should I speak?
> I stand dishonoured that have gone about
> To link my dear friend to a common stale.   *(lines 57–9)*

Don John, cleverly keeping a low profile, says just enough to make matters even worse and Benedick realises that things are seriously wrong:

LEONATO Are these things spoken, or do I but dream?
DON JOHN Sir, they are spoken, and these things are true.
BENEDICK This looks not like a nuptial.
HERO   True, oh God!   *(lines 60–2)*

In one production the shocked onlookers echoed Don John's 'true!' to add to Hero's sense of nightmare. Her sense of isolation is further heightened when even her own father seems to doubt her. It seems as though every man in the congregation is accusing her, demanding that she give answers to their questions. Not even Beatrice has felt able to come to her defence. Claudio now confronts Hero with the 'truth' of what he has seen. Her very 'name' (reputation) is at stake. Did she or did she not talk with a man at her bedroom window the previous night? Her denial is brushed aside by both Don Pedro and Don John, who each confirm Claudio's accusation. They too have seen her with their own eyes talking with another man at her window and heard him speak of their many previous secret encounters.

Where is Margaret, who could testify to the falsehood of the whole affair? She is not named in the script as one of those present, but would surely have been there to watch her mistress get married. She has often been shown making a quick exit, as if ashamed of what she has done. One production ingeniously had Don John step in front of Margaret as she came forward to confess the truth. He slid open his walking stick to reveal a dagger hidden inside, the threat enough to ensure her silence.

Claudio takes his farewell of Hero in verse full of bitter wordplay:

> But fare thee well, most foul, most fair, farewell
> Thou pure impiety, and impious purity,
> For thee I'll lock up all the gates of love,
> And on my eyelids shall conjecture hang,
> To turn all beauty into thoughts of harm,
> And never shall it more be gracious.   *(lines 96–101)*

Claudio's anguish at the gulf between the 'real' Hero and the 'seeming' Hero, is expressed in oxymorons (two contradictory ideas placed side by side): 'foul' – 'fair'; 'pure impiety' – 'impious purity'. The verse is powerfully emotional, yet some critics feel the very artificiality of its patterning suggests a shallowness in Claudio's feelings. His grief is not for Hero but more for himself and his own loss of honour.

Leonato's response to Claudio's farewell speech brings matters to a crisis. Just when Hero needed her father's support most of all, he too judges her guilty, concerned only for his own shame and loss of honour. It is all too much for Hero to bear and she faints. Several late twentieth-century productions have highlighted the male–female divisions at this crucial moment. One had Hero surrounded by Beatrice and the other women, while the men moved away nursing their grievances.

Don John (wisely from his point of view) suggests to Claudio and Don Pedro that this would be a good moment to leave, which they do. Benedick now has a crucial decision to make. Does he leave with his friends, or stay with the woman he loves? He stays. Some feminist critics see this as the key moment which begins Benedick's rejection of male companionship and values (see page 97).

When Hero begins to regain consciousness, Shakespeare focuses not on her but her father. Leonato clearly believes his daughter guilty of Claudio's accusations and wishes heartily that she were dead. He is ashamed of her and heartbroken that his only child has so defiled both herself and him:

> Do not live, Hero, do not ope thine eyes   (line 116)

Like Claudio's farewell speech, Leonato's words are powerfully patterned to express anger at his only child and pity for himself, constantly repeating 'I' and 'mine'. There are no fewer than 14 self-references in just five lines (lines 127–31). He wishes that he had never had a daughter but had adopted instead some beggar's child so that he could now feel no part of her shame:

> Why had I not with charitable hand,
> Took up a beggar's issue at my gates,
> Who smirchèd thus, and mired with infamy,

I might have said, no part of it is mine,
This shame derives itself from unknown loins:
But mine, and mine I loved, and mine I praised,
And mine that I was proud on, mine so much,
That I myself, was to myself not mine,
Valuing of her: why she, oh she is fallen
Into a pit of ink, that the wide sea
Hath drops too few to wash her clean again   *(lines 124–34)*

As with Claudio's earlier speech, many have detected a rather undignified excess of self-pity and resentment in Leonato's words. Some eighteenth- and nineteenth-century productions cut part of this speech in an attempt to make him seem a more sympathetic character. More recent twentieth-century productions, however, have highlighted the violence of his words, so similar to Capulet's verbal violence towards his daughter in *Romeo and Juliet*.

Benedick is amazed by all the accusations and 'evidence' of guilt, and cannot find words to express his feelings. The only one to keep faith with Hero is Beatrice, for she knows in her *heart* that her cousin is innocent:

BENEDICK Sir, sir, be patient. For my part I am so attired in wonder,
    I know not what to say.
BEATRICE Oh on my soul my cousin is belied.   *(lines 137–9)*

In contrast to Beatrice, all the other characters in the play desperately attempt to discover the truth by 'noting' the outward signs. Leonato, for example, has noted Claudio and Don Pedro's evidence and condemned Hero. When Beatrice says that she had not slept with Hero the previous night, it only confirms his conviction. Yet Leonato does not stop to think about the significance of her statement that she had been Hero's bedfellow every night for the previous 12 months. Friar Francis has also been 'noting of the lady' (line 150), and the outward signs he sees convince him that Hero is innocent.

Nonetheless, Leonato still refuses to believe his daughter's innocence, even though she continues to protest it. In desperation she declares that Leonato can torture her to death if Claudio's accusations are proved true and her passionate protestations at last provoke the men to think more rationally. The Friar feels that Don Pedro and Don

John may have been mistaken. Benedick rightly suspects that it is Don John who is at the bottom of it all:

FRIAR FRANCIS There is some strange misprision in the princes.
BENEDICK Two of them have the very bent of honour,
    And if their wisdoms be misled in this,
    The practice of it lives in John the bastard,
    Whose spirits toil in frame of villainies.   *(lines 178–82)*

Even Leonato now entertains the possibility that his daughter might not be guilty and vows revenge on her accusers if it is proved 'they wrong her honour'. At which point, the Friar outlines a plan which may put matters right. Let it be thought that Hero has indeed died and put on a formal show of mourning. The news of her death may cause her accusers to feel some pity and even make Claudio realise how much he really loved her. If that fails, at least Hero can be hidden away under a new name in some secluded religious house.

Benedick now decides where his honour lies. Although his love and loyalty is very much with the prince and Claudio, he swears on his honour to support Leonato and advises him to follow the Friar's plan. Leonato, too grief-stricken to object, departs with Hero and the Friar. Only Beatrice and Benedick remain. Beatrice feels deeply for Hero and is furious at Claudio's treatment of her. Benedick is moved by Beatrice's unhappiness and concern for her friend. There is a new hesitancy and a gentleness in their speech:

BENEDICK Lady Beatrice, have you wept all this while?
BEATRICE Yea, and I will weep a little longer.
BENEDICK I will not desire that.
BEATRICE You have no reason, I do it freely.
BENEDICK Surely I do believe your fair cousin is wronged.
BEATRICE Ah, how much might the man deserve of me that would
    right her!
BENEDICK Is there any way to show such friendship?
BEATRICE A very even way, but no such friend.
BENEDICK May a man do it?
BEATRICE It is a man's office, but not yours.   *(lines 248–58)*

What Beatrice is hinting at here is that she desperately needs a man to challenge Claudio in defence of Hero's honour. The aristocratic code of honour demanded that such a challenge to single combat be made by a man of the family, which may be why at first she rejects Benedick's offer of help. She may also believe that his friendship with Claudio will compel him to refuse.

Benedick, as yet unaware of where her words are leading him, summons up his courage to confess his love for her (one Benedick looked round to check no one was listening before he committed himself). Beatrice wants to return his love but hesitates, for Benedick is the close friend of her deadliest enemy:

BENEDICK I do love nothing in the world so well as you, is not that
      strange?
BEATRICE As strange as the thing I know not: it were as possible for
      me to say, I loved nothing so well as you, but believe me not,
      and yet I lie not, I confess nothing, nor I deny nothing: I am
      sorry for my cousin.   *(lines 259–64)*

Her evasive and equivocal reply, reveals just enough for Benedick to suspect that she does indeed love him. He is delighted, and speaks to her for the first time in the play using the intimate 'thou'. But Beatrice is not yet ready to commit herself and her wordplay now has a deadly purpose. When Benedick swears by his sword, she warns him not to 'swear and eat it' (meaning 'do not go back on your oath' or perhaps 'do not eat your sword by getting yourself wounded in combat'), for she knows that if she accepts Benedick, her duty must be to ask her future husband to challenge Claudio. To accept Benedick's love is to risk his death:

BENEDICK By my sword, Beatrice, thou lovest me.
BEATRICE Do not swear and eat it.
BENEDICK I will swear by it that you love me, and I will make him
      eat it that says I love not you.
BEATRICE Will you not eat your word?
BENEDICK With no sauce that can be devised to it: I protest I love
      thee.
BEATRICE Why then God forgive me.
BENEDICK What offence, sweet Beatrice?

BEATRICE You have stayed me in a happy hour, I was about to
        protest I loved you.
BENEDICK And do it with all thy heart.
BEATRICE I love you with so much of my heart, that none is left to
        protest.
BENEDICK Come bid me do anything for thee.
BEATRICE Kill Claudio.
BENEDICK Ha, not for the wide world.
BEATRICE You kill me to deny it, farewell.   *(lines 265–81)*

Beatrice's famous command to 'Kill Claudio' has been delivered in
a variety of ways. Some Beatrices have spoken with a savage force and
deadly intensity. Others have spoken it as half-appeal, half-command.
One Beatrice paused as if throwing down a challenge to Benedick
which she feared might end their relationship.

Benedick's response to her demand ('Ha, not for the wide world')
has been delivered in equally various ways. Some have reacted in an
incredulous way that invited laughter, as if the request were too
ridiculous for words. Others have shown in their response the
realisation that they really *were* being asked to 'do anything' for
Beatrice and were going to have to choose between friendship and the
woman they loved.

The problem for the actors in this sequence is that, despite
Beatrice's outrage at the despicable treatment of Hero, the
extravagance and surprise of her demand to 'Kill Claudio' is
potentially comic and the line sometimes draws laughter from the
audience, as does Benedick's response. Yet Beatrice's declaration of
what his answer means to her ('You kill me to deny it') is no
exaggeration. It is deeply and seriously meant. Many productions have
therefore sought to achieve a knife-edge balance between the comic
and the serious in this climactic scene.

In most productions Beatrice has attempted to leave at this point
and been restrained by Benedick as he attempts to win back her good
favour. Prevented from leaving, Beatrice makes her feelings
abundantly clear. All her anger at Claudio's treatment of Hero,
combined with years of frustration at living in a man's world explodes
at once. How *dare* Claudio wait until the public spotlight of the
wedding to make his slanderous accusations:

Is a not approved in the height a villain, that hath slandered, scorned, dishonoured my kinswoman? Oh that I were a man! What, bear her in hand, until they come to take hands, and then with public accusation, uncovered slander, unmitigated rancour? Oh God that I were a man! I would eat his heart in the market place.   *(lines 291–5)*

Once again, Beatrice has the last thrust in the wordplay: if she were a man she would eat neither her word nor her sword. She would eat Claudio's *heart*. Benedick attempts to speak, but Beatrice's anger, frustration and despair will not be halted – yet. Eventually, however, she subsides somewhat to allow Benedick to ask one final question:

BENEDICK Think you in your soul the Count Claudio hath wronged
     Hero?
BEATRICE Yea, as sure as I have a thought, or a soul.   *(lines 310–12)*

This is 'truth' enough for Benedick. He pledges his word that he will challenge Claudio and his commitment to the women's cause is absolute: 'I am engaged'.

Act 4 Scene 2

The mood shifts from near-tragedy back to comedy again as Dogberry and Verges begin their 'examination' of Borachio and Conrade. Acting as scribe is the Sexton. Dogberry attempts to conduct proceedings in what he believes is the correct manner, but neither he nor Verges have any idea of how to go about it and the Sexton has to keep prompting them what to do. Their comically inadequate grasp of the language is once again apparent. When the Sexton asks them who the 'malefactors' are, Dogberry assumes it is himself and Verges!

Dogberry begins his cross-examination well enough, asking Borachio and Conrade their names and whether they 'serve God'. Then he attempts a cunning piece of legal trickery. First he accuses the two men of being 'false knaves' and asks them to reply. Conrade denies the charge. Then Dogberry takes Borachio aside and whispers into his ear the same accusation. When Borachio gives the same answer, Dogberry is baffled. Since they have both given the same answer they *must* be telling the truth! Mercifully, the Sexton knows better how to conduct an examination and instructs Dogberry to call the Watch to give their evidence.

Seacoal, the first man to give evidence, has obviously failed to understand the significance of what he saw and he accuses Borachio of calling Don John a villain. Dogberry seizes on this as being the crime of 'flat perjury' (downright lying) because, in Dogberry's eyes, a prince's brother could never be a villain.

Once again, the Sexton has to intervene to get at the real truth. He asks a second Watchman what else he saw. This man is more sharp-witted and reports that Borachio said he had 'received a thousand ducats of Don John, for accusing the Lady Hero wrongfully'. Dogberry and Verges nod wisely – the crime is obviously burglary! Ignoring these buffoons, the Sexton pursues the matter. What else did the two accused say? Seacoal tells him that when Count Claudio heard Borachio's words he said would disgrace Hero before the whole church assembly and refuse to marry her. Dogberry is horrified, but as usual muddles his words, mistaking 'redemption' for 'damnation':

> Oh villain! Thou wilt be condemned into everlasting
> redemption for this.   *(lines 47–8)*

Fortunately, the Sexton realises the significance of Seacoal's evidence. He knows that Don John had 'secretly stolen away' that morning, that Hero had been accused in exactly the manner the watchmen reported and had died from the shock and shame. He orders Borachio and Conrade to be bound and taken to Leonato's.

Conrade, exasperated beyond endurance, calls Dogberry a 'coxcomb' (fool) and an 'ass'. Dogberry is mortally offended. He has been called an ass, but there is no one to write it down as evidence! Like Hero, his good name has been defamed and he wants justice:

> Oh that he were here to write me down an ass! But masters,
> remember that I am an ass, though it be not written down, yet
> forget not that I am an ass   *(lines 62–4)*

So Dogberry marshals up all his dignity. He lists his many virtues then, seething with indignation at the insult he has received, ends with yet another reminder of the affront to his self-esteem:

> oh that I had been writ down an ass!   *(lines 70–1)*

Act 4: Critical review

The play's double plot comes to a double crisis, sending the audience on a rollercoaster ride of emotions, from Hero's cruel denunciation, through Beatrice and Benedick's intensely intimate conversation, to the comic trial which somehow manages to get to the truth. Yet, for all the fluctuations of feeling, Shakespeare's focus remains clear: can we ever be sure we know truth from appearance?

Characters who had earlier played with deception now search in earnest for the truth. Claudio is convinced that Hero's maiden-like blushes are 'exterior shows', her honour merely 'seeming' purity. His certainty even convinces Leonato because, in his judgement, men of honour do not lie. When Leonato 'notes' Claudio's tears, he interprets them as a sign of the young man's sincerity. The irony is that both men are deceived, not just by Don John but by their own male valuation of women: loss of virginity means loss of worth.

The Friar, in contrast, 'notes' carefully the same events and concludes that Hero is innocent. His plan to find out the truth involves yet another deception. Hero must pretend to die, thereby prompting Claudio to realise how much he really loved her.

But Beatrice knows the truth instinctively. Hero has been 'belied' (slandered). Beatrice's distress and concern for her cousin brings the second plot to its crisis. Benedick, touched by her predicament, abandons his former friendship with Claudio and Don Pedro, pledging his life for Beatrice's love and for the honour of her friend. Unlike Claudio and Leonato, there is no pretence or delusion in their words. They speak from the heart.

The pain of the near-tragic events at the church is immediately eased by Dogberry and Verges' comic attempts to get at the truth in their 'examination' of Borachio and Conrade. Any fear that they might never do so is allayed by the Sexton's sharp intelligence. The audience knows the crisis will soon be resolved.

Dogberry's display of wounded pride on being called an ass gives a final comic echo to Claudio's earlier more serious outpouring of wounded honour. Dogberry, too, is obsessively concerned with appearance and, like Claudio, is deeply offended by what he sees as an insult to his status and dignity.

Act 5 Scene 1

The loss of his daughter's reputation continues to hit Leonato hard. His brother Antonio attempts to comfort him but Leonato refuses to be consoled. Only a man who has loved and cherished a daughter and suffered a similar injustice is entitled to give him counsel. It is easy to preach patience to others, but no man can practise what he preaches when tragedy strikes him personally.

Many productions have heavily cut Leonato's speech, possibly feeling that he is being too self-indulgent in his grief. His daughter is not dead and the love he claims to feel for Hero was hardly evident at the church. Yet, in a sense, Hero is dead to him, for in Messina's patriarchal society a woman who has lost her good name is nothing.

Leonato is more receptive to Antonio's suggestion that he turn his mind to thoughts of revenge. In words which echo Beatrice's words spoken at the church, Leonato declares that Hero was falsely accused:

> My soul doth tell me, Hero is belied   *(line 42)*

The appearance of Don Pedro and Claudio, hastening past in search of Benedick and apparently unconcerned about the grief they have caused him, provokes Leonato beyond endurance. He sarcastically questions their haste to be away (they had agreed to stay for a month), then accuses Claudio, calling him a 'dissembler' (deceiver), no longer using the polite 'you' but the insulting 'thou'. Despite his age, Leonato challenges Claudio to single combat for the false accusation which has caused his daughter to die of shame. Yet still Claudio and the prince seem to feel no sense of guilt or responsibility for what they have done. Several productions have had them respond in a sneering, almost brutal manner, as if they had caught Leonato out trying to sell them inferior merchandise.

Again, the play hovers on the edge of tragedy. Some productions have interpreted this sequence as the desperate challenge of an aged father whose daughter's life has been destroyed. These Leonatos have slapped Claudio's face, struck him and held a sword to his throat. Other productions, in contrast, have underlined the absurdity of the old man's challenge, turning it into an undignified scuffle, with one Leonato trying to draw his sword but unable even to get it out of the scabbard.

When Claudio refuses to fight with Leonato, Antonio also challenges him, with a contempt ('Sir Boy') and taunting ferocity that surprises even Leonato. Antonio's challenge to Claudio has almost invariably been presented in comic fashion. One Antonio threw an umbrella at Claudio while chasing him around the stage. Another, in a paroxysm of senile fury, chased him with a stick. Another was so enraged by the time he had finished that he collapsed with a seizure and Don Pedro had to help him up.

Even now, neither the prince nor Claudio show any sense of remorse. Don Pedro's defence is sincerely meant, but to the audience, who know the truth, his words have a hollow ring:

> Gentlemen both, we will not wake your patience,
> My heart is sorry for your daughter's death:
> But on my honour she was charged with nothing
> But what was true, and very full of proof.   *(lines 101–4)*

Leonato begs to speak further on the matter but the prince is adamant – he will not hear another word. The two old men leave, still rumbling indignantly.

Don Pedro and Claudio regard the arrival of Benedick as welcome light relief, unaware of the deadly mission he is on. Many Benedicks have made their serious intent clear from the start, ignoring Claudio's greeting and addressing their 'Good day, my lord' coldly to Don Pedro only. Benedick shakes off the jests of his former friends with a cool dignity that contrasts strongly with their unfeeling flippancy. In one production Claudio was about to slap Benedick on the back at line 127 ('What, courage, man'), but changed his mind when he saw the look in Benedick's eye. Eventually Benedick takes Claudio aside to issue his challenge and offer Claudio the choice of venue and weapons:

BENEDICK Shall I speak a word in your ear?
CLAUDIO God bless me from a challenge.
BENEDICK You are a villain, I jest not, I will make it good how you
    dare, with what you dare, and when you dare: do me right, or
    I will protest your cowardice: you have killed a sweet lady,
    and her death shall fall heavy on you: let me hear from you.
CLAUDIO Well I will meet you, so I may have good cheer.
DON PEDRO What, a feast, a feast?   *(lines 135–42)*

Even at this critical point comedy mingles with tragedy. Either Don Pedro is deliberately mocking, or he has heard only the final part of Claudio's acceptance of the challenge, for he assumes the two men are planning a celebratory meal.

But Claudio's subsequent threat to carve Benedick's 'calf's head' and 'capon' to 'find a woodcock' (all stupid defenceless animals) is ominously clear. He too means business. Sensing things are dangerously tense, Don Pedro tries to fill the uneasy silence, relating at length all the mocking things Beatrice had recently said about Benedick and how she had confessed she loved him despite everything. Perhaps the pressure of events is also getting to the prince because he even makes a crass reference to the dead Hero, claiming 'the old man's daughter told us all'.

Claudio joins Don Pedro in mocking Benedick for falling in love, hinting at the trick they have played on him, their jokes about cuckolded husbands deliberately echoing Benedick's own comments in the opening scene about 'the savage bull' and 'Benedick the married man'. But Benedick remains unmoved. He takes his leave, but not before repeating his challenge to Claudio and resigning from Don Pedro's service.

Although left in no doubt that Benedick's challenge is in earnest, the prince and Claudio find his actions incomprehensibly foolish, until Don Pedro recalls something Benedick said, which sows the first seeds of doubt in his mind:

> But soft you, let me be, pluck up my heart, and be sad, did he
> not say my brother was fled? *(lines 183–4)*

Before they can fully grasp the significance of this, Dogberry, Verges and the Watch enter with their prisoners, Borachio and Conrade. It is characteristic once again of Shakespeare's mingling of the comic and serious that proof of Hero's innocence should be delivered by such incompetents. Dogberry lists six virtually identical crimes in perplexingly random numerical order. Not to be outdone, the prince repeats his question in similar style:

DOGBERRY Marry, sir, they have committed false report, moreover
    they have spoken untruths, secondarily, they are slanders,
    sixth and lastly, they have belied a lady, thirdly they have

> verified unjust things, and to conclude, they are lying knaves.
> DON PEDRO First I ask you what they have done, thirdly I ask thee
>   what's their offence, sixth and lastly why they are committed,
>   and to conclude, what you lay to their charge?   *(lines 191–7)*

Dogberry is silent. The baffler has been outbaffled (one Dogberry swayed precariously with a confused look on his face). So Don Pedro asks the prisoners themselves what they have done, remarking sarcastically that the 'learned constable' is too clever to be understood.

Borachio immediately confesses everything, perhaps out of genuine remorse, or hoping thereby to be treated more leniently. As he gives his account of the deception, his words, like his remarks on the 'deformed thief' fashion in Act 3 Scene 3, echo one of the central preoccupations of the play: the problem of distinguishing truth from illusion, appearance from reality. He confirms how easily he had deceived even the eyes of Don Pedro and Claudio, how they saw him 'court Margaret in Hero's garments' and how it took two uneducated idiots to bring the truth to light when all their learned wisdom failed (Dogberry and Verges have often beamed with pleasure at this compliment). Borachio's apparently heartfelt confession is not entirely truthful. He claims Don John 'incensed [him] to slander the Lady Hero' when in fact he devised the entire plot himself (Act 2 Scene 2).

The effect of Borachio's confession on Don Pedro and Claudio is devastating:

> DON PEDRO Runs not this speech like iron through your blood?
> CLAUDIO I have drunk poison whiles he uttered it.   *(lines 214–15)*

Leonato returns with his brother and the Sexton. He knows the truth about Hero's slander and is understandably angry and vengeful, yet strangely forgiving, for he has one final deception in mind through which he hopes to bring about a happy resolution to the near-tragedy. Still maintaining the pretence that Hero is dead, he first confronts Borachio with his crime, then sarcastically thanks Claudio and Don Pedro for their 'high and worthy deeds'. The prince and Claudio are deeply ashamed and ask what penance they can do to make amends.

Leonato prescribes their tasks. They are to announce to all Messina that Hero was completely innocent and make a public show of repentance that night at her tomb. His final requirement is unusual to say the least. The following morning Claudio must agree to marry Antonio's daughter, a woman almost the twin of Hero and heir to both their fortunes. That done, Leonato will regard his revenge as being satisfied. Claudio accepts wholeheartedly. Again mingling the comic and serious, several productions have had Antonio do a double-take at the mention of his non-existent daughter (line 255), as if Leonato's plan was a surprise to him as well. Leonato now turns to Margaret, whom he believes was part of the conspiracy. Borachio, however, assures him that she was entirely innocent and unaware of what was going on.

Having begun on the verge of tragedy, the scene ends on a comic note. Dogberry has other important information to report and it will take more than a prince, a count and a governor to silence him. Firstly, Conrade called him an ass, and secondly there is another villain called Deformed still at large. Borachio's sardonic remark about that 'deformed thief' fashion, which the Watch thought was a local thief who wore his hair in a lovelock, has now become, in Dogberry's addled brain, a notorious villain who keeps a key in his ear with a padlock hanging down beside it!

All a bemused Leonato can do is thank Dogberry and Verges for their work and reward them. Eventually Dogberry and Verges leave, but not before Dogberry has wished Leonato well at least five times in his own uniquely garbled way:

> God keep your worship, I wish your worship well, God restore
> you to health, I humbly give you leave to depart, and if a
> merry meeting may be wished, God prohibit it: come,
> neighbour.   *(lines 286–9)*

Don Pedro and Claudio leave to prepare to mount a vigil at Hero's monument, promising to meet with Leonato the next morning. Leonato and Antonio leave to speak with Margaret about her association with Borachio.

Act 5 Scene 2

Shakespeare now switches the audience's attention back to the Beatrice–Benedick plot. Benedick asks for Margaret's help in arranging a meeting with Beatrice. As she did earlier with Beatrice,

Margaret attempts to match wits with Benedick in playfully bawdy language, full of sexual innuendo. She seems strangely unconcerned about the part she has played in Hero's slander.

After Margaret has departed to fetch Beatrice, Benedick has a last minute practice at singing a love song. The ideal Elizabethan courtier was both soldier and poet. Songs, sonnets and blank verse were traditional ways for a lover to express his love. However, Benedick's attempt at singing is by his own admission 'pitiful', as are his attempts at writing poetry. But that does not mean his love is not deep. He tells the audience that all the smooth, blank-verse-speaking lovers of history (Leander, Troilus, etc.)

> were never so truly turned over and over as my poor self in
> love   *(lines 26–7)*

His soliloquy is interrupted by Beatrice and their 'merry war' resumes, but with new playfulness and mutual sympathy:

BENEDICK Sweet Beatrice, wouldst thou come when I called thee?
BEATRICE Yea, signor, and depart when you bid me.
BENEDICK Oh stay but till then.
BEATRICE Then, is spoken: fare you well now   *(lines 32–5)*

Benedick confirms that he has challenged Claudio, then asks Beatrice to tell him what had made her fall in love with him. There seems a certain defensiveness in her answer. She deflects his question with a joke, puts the same question to him, which he in turn parries. All of which leads Benedick to conclude

> Thou and I are too wise to woo peaceably.   *(line 54)*

Yet for all their defensiveness there is a genuine desire for love. Beatrice even encourages Benedick to continue with his mock-serious praising of his own virtues, while he in turn expresses a genuine concern for her cousin and herself:

BENEDICK . . . so much for praising myself, who I myself will bear
    witness is praiseworthy: and now tell me, how doth your
    cousin?

BEATRICE Very ill.

BENEDICK And how do you?

BEATRICE Very ill too.

BENEDICK Serve God, love me, and mend: there will I leave you too,
    for here comes one in haste.   *(lines 65–72)*

It is Ursula entering with the news that Don John's plot has been
uncovered and Hero's good name restored. Beatrice and Benedick's
new happiness is aptly summed up in the comic, self-deprecating
anticlimax of Benedick's final declaration of love:

BEATRICE Will you go hear this news, signor?

BENEDICK I will live in thy heart, die in thy lap, and be buried in thy
    eyes: and moreover, I will go with thee to thy uncle's.

(lines 77–9)

Act 5 Scene 3

It is night and, as they promised, Claudio and Don Pedro arrive at
Hero's monument to keep their vigil. A tribute to Hero is read out, a
solemn hymn sung and a vow made to commemorate each future
anniversary of her death.

Claudio's act of penitence marks an important transition in the
play from the darkness of the denunciation scene in the church to the
happiness and festivities of the denouement. The solemn ritual of this
scene, coupled with music, singing, movement and (in modern times)
lighting effects, makes for powerfully moving theatre. In one
production, the lights dimmed, a tomb-like monument rose up from
beneath the stage and shadowy figures entered, bearing flickering
torches. In Henry Irving's nineteenth-century production, a torchlit
procession of monks and black-robed mourners entered, a funeral bell
tolled and a choir sang 'Pardon, goddess of the night', the music
continuing softly as background to the spoken words. Branagh's film
showed a spectacular torchlit procession moving in the darkness up
the mountainside.

Many productions have given the Lord's lines (3–10 and 22–3) to
Claudio, which has allowed him to make a moving show of grief.
Others have argued that since he wooed Hero by proxy, he would
probably grieve by proxy also. Hero's epitaph, with its regular metre
and end-stopped lines, has a cold, almost frozen quality as if the

language itself were dead, while the short rhyming couplets of the song sound almost like an incantation.

In Act 4, the play moved from light into darkness. Now, with the completion of the ceremony and the coming of dawn, it moves back from darkness into light. Since Elizabethan theatres lacked lighting effects, dramatists often signalled such changes with language, and so Don Pedro instructs the attendants to extinguish their torches thus:

> Good morrow, masters, put your torches out,
> The wolves have preyed, and look, the gentle day
> Before the wheels of Phoebus, round about
> Dapples the drowsy east with spots of grey　　　　*(lines 24–7)*

Claudio and Don Pedro leave to change out of their mourning dress and into wedding clothes, ready to fulfil the final part of Claudio's promise – to marry Antonio's daughter.

Act 5 Scene 4

The final scene of the play (just 120 lines) brings the Hero–Claudio and Beatrice–Benedick plots to a surprisingly swift conclusion. Leonato and his household (minus Beatrice), together with Benedick and the Friar, await the arrival of Claudio and Don Pedro. Leonato seems to have forgiven Claudio, Don Pedro, and even Margaret for their part in the near-tragedy. Now, in a manner very reminiscent of the masked deception scene in Act 2 Scene 1, he sets in motion his plan for the wedding of Claudio to Antonio's daughter. Hero and the other gentlewomen are sent away to mask themselves in readiness for the ceremony.

Benedick also has wedding plans. He tells Leonato and the Friar that he wishes to marry Beatrice. Despite Benedick's evident seriousness of intention, Leonato cannot resist hinting at the deceptions he and his friends have played on him and Beatrice. His remarks leave Benedick momentarily baffled:

> Your answer, sir, is enigmatical,
> But for my will, my will is, your good will
> May stand with ours, this day to be conjoined,
> In the state of honourable marriage,
> In which (good friar) I shall desire your help.　　　*(lines 27–31)*

To suggest that he is wanting to marry almost in spite of himself, several Benedicks have had trouble even speaking the dreaded m-word. One stammered out, 'In the state of honourable m-m-m-marriage'.

Claudio and Don Pedro enter and Leonato asks Claudio if he is ready to honour his promise to marry Antonio's daughter. Claudio's reply, 'I'll hold my mind were she an Ethiop' sounds racist to modern ears, but would have passed unremarked in Elizabethan times when pale skin was seen as a mark of beauty (see page 65).

While they wait for the arrival of the bride, the prince and Claudio look to have some fun at Benedick's expense. Claudio mocks his new-found love of marriage, likening his cuckold's horns to those of the god Jove when he disguised himself as a bull to seduce the princess Europa. But Benedick cannot so easily forget past injuries. His reply is wittily brutal, the couplet form giving it an epigrammatic sharpness. Claudio's mother, he says, must also have been seen to by some strange bull because Claudio makes the same bleating calf noises:

> Bull Jove, sir, had an amiable low,
> And some such strange bull leaped your father's cow,
> And got a calf in that same noble feat,
> Much like to you, for you have just his bleat. *(lines 48–51)*

These exchanges may echo the men's friendly joking in the opening scene, but there is also a bitterness and hostility in their words which has prompted many productions (like the Branagh film) to either abridge or cut the sequence to preserve an atmosphere of reconciliation and forgiveness.

Benedick and Claudio are forced to put aside their differences when Antonio enters with four masked ladies (Hero, Beatrice, Margaret and Ursula). This second betrothal scene echoes the first, but in a strange, ritualistic way, for this betrothal is more like a rebirth: the creation of a new Hero and a new Claudio. Claudio's acceptance of his masked bride demonstrates the truth of his love for Hero, while Hero unmasks to reveal the truth of her chastity:

CLAUDIO Give me your hand before this holy friar,
     I am your husband if you like of me.
HERO And when I lived I was your other wife,

And when you loved, you were my other husband. (*She unmasks*)

CLAUDIO Another Hero?

HERO   Nothing certainer.
    One Hero died defiled, but I do live,
    And surely as I live, I am a maid.   *(lines 58–64)*

But Benedick has yet to find *his* wife. He assumes one of the other masked ladies is Beatrice, but which? Several Benedicks have gone up and down the line trying to find her; one Beatrice kept changing places to avoid being discovered. The process of unmasking for Beatrice and Benedick, however, is not simply a matter of removing a disguise. They also have a deeply ingrained psychological barrier to overcome. Declaring their love privately is one thing, making a public commitment to marriage is another. Neither wants to be the first to admit their love wholeheartedy before witnesses, so instead they revert to their old joking denial of affection:

BENEDICK Do not you love me?

BEATRICE   Why no, no more than reason.

BENEDICK Why then your uncle, and the prince, and Claudio,
    Have been deceived, they swore you did.

BEATRICE Do not you love me?

BENEDICK   Troth no, no more than reason.

(lines 74–7)

At which point, Claudio and Hero produce love sonnets written secretly by each about the other. Usually Beatrice and Benedick have snatched at the sonnet written about them to read it delightedly (one Beatrice peered at the paper shortsightedly while a long-sighted Benedick held his at arm's length). Both are now convinced of the other's love and agree to marry, yet still they cannot resist a little affectionate one-upmanship, claiming to be marrying the other only out of pity:

BENEDICK A miracle, here's our own hands against our hearts: come,
    I will have thee, but by this light I take thee for pity.

BEATRICE I would not deny you, but by this good day, I yield upon
    great persuasion, and partly to save your life, for I was told,
    you were in a consumption.   *(lines 91–5)*

But Benedick ends the exchange with a kiss:

> Peace I will stop your mouth.   *(line 96)*

It is the convention in a comedy that all differences are eventually resolved, so Beatrice and Benedick's kiss would seem to indicate their future happiness. But Beatrice's silence (she says no more in the play, while Benedick dominates proceedings) worries some critics. Does she accept marriage unreservedly? Her love for Benedick may be strong, but, as she herself remarked in Act 2 Scene 1, marriage is for life and happiness is not guaranteed.

Benedick, however, does embrace marriage wholeheartedly. When Don Pedro teasingly asks him what it is like to be married (in one production all the male characters made horns and went 'Moo'), Benedick is unabashed at his change of heart (lines 98–104) and even seeks to be reconciled with Claudio, despite the latter's tactless prophecy that he will prove an unfaithful husband. Many productions have played the reconciliation with friendliness and forgiveness, although, in the 1990 Royal Shakespeare Company's production, Claudio's sneering comment almost provoked Benedick to violence, had not Beatrice restrained him. Claudio in return was very reluctant to shake Benedick's hand when he said, 'Come, come, we are friends', as if their old comradeship would never be the same again.

Benedick insists that the whole company dance to lighten their hearts before the double marriage ceremony, and even advises the prince to get himself married. Not even the arrival of a messenger with news of Don John's capture can stop Benedick:

> Think not on him till tomorrow, I'll devise thee brave
> punishments for him: strike up, pipers.   *(lines 119–20)*

The play has traditionally ended with music and dancing to create a mood of romantic harmony and reconciliation, but modern productions have sometimes ended more sombrely, for example isolating Don Pedro as a melancholy, wistful onlooker (notice Benedick's remark 'Prince, thou art sad, get thee a wife'). At the end of the Branagh film there was a chilling moment when Don John was brought back to face his brother, and the two men looked at each other with hate in their eyes.

Act 5: Critical review

Claudio's public denunciation of Hero has severely shaken the comfortable world of Messina. Leonato can scarcely bring himself to address Don Pedro politely. Both he and his brother challenge Claudio, as does Benedick, who then resigns from the prince's service. Borachio's confession that Hero was the victim of a cruel deceit devastates Claudio and the prince. They beg Leonato to exact whatever revenge he chooses.

Leonato might have reacted harshly, but instead initiates one final deception, which brings about the play's resolution. Claudio and Don Pedro must do penance by publicly admitting their slanderous accusations and mourning Hero's death that night at her tomb. Finally, Claudio must marry Antonio's daughter. Weeping with remorse, Claudio gratefully accepts Leonato's terms.

Benedick meanwhile seeks to speak privately with Beatrice. Neither songs nor poetry can hope to win such an independent woman, only courage in an honourable cause. But his challenge to Claudio has clearly opened the way to Beatrice's heart.

Claudio and the prince's vigil at Hero's tomb is another turning point in the drama, literally the darkness before the dawn. It is theatrically unlike anything else in the play, a still, cold, frozen moment of grief and regret, which the approaching sunrise turns to hope.

The play's resolution is swift. Claudio must re-enact the wedding ceremony he so cruelly aborted, so that a 'new' Hero can be born. It is as if the regenerative power of Providence and Nature, together with forgiveness and repentance, has renewed their marriage. In a reversal of the earlier masked dance and betrothal, Hero unmasks to reveal her 'true' identity, as does Beatrice. She and Benedick confess their love and publicly agree to marry.

To symbolise their final harmony, the betrothed couples dance unmasked, for the first time seeing 'truly'. This conclusion arouses complicated responses in an audience, as some ask: for whom does marriage constitute a happy ending? Is Hero happy? Is Beatrice? The uncertainty is typically Shakespearian. His comedies show that to celebrate happiness, life and fertility, and at the same time acknowledge loss and pain, is to reflect the reality of life.

Contexts

This section identifies the contexts from which *Much Ado About Nothing* emerged: the wide range of different influences which fostered the creativity of Shakespeare as he wrote the play. These contexts ensured that *Much Ado About Nothing* is full of all kinds of reminders of everyday life, and the familiar knowledge, assumptions, beliefs and values of Elizabethan England.

What did Shakespeare write?

Scholars generally agree that *Much Ado About Nothing* was written in the latter part of 1598. Shakespeare's original manuscript has not survived, but the first printed version of the play, the Quarto edition of 1600, was probably based closely on it, because it has a few inconsistencies of the kind that often occur in an author's original draft. Some give glimpses of how Shakespeare's mind worked. For example, the name of Imogen, Leonato's wife, appears in the list of characters for Act 1 Scene 1 and Act 2 Scene 1, but she is given no dialogue and thereafter disappears from the play. Some critics have suggested that Shakespeare removed the mother to accentuate the pathos of Hero's isolation in Act 4 Scene 1. The names of Shakespeare's company comedians, Kemp and Cowley, appear as speech headings instead of Dogberry and Verges in Act 4 Scene 2, evidence that Shakespeare wrote at least some of his parts with particular actors in mind.

A version of *Much Ado About Nothing* was included in the First Folio edition of Shakespeare's plays (1623), published seven years after his death. However, most modern editions of the play are based on the Quarto text, it being judged closer to Shakespeare's original. Even so, the edition of the play you are using will vary in many minor respects from other editions. This is because, although most editors use the Quarto version, each one makes a multitude of different judgements about such matters as spelling, punctuation, stage directions (entrances, exits, asides, etc.), scene locations and other features.

So the text of *Much Ado About Nothing* is not as stable as you might think. This is no reason for dismay, but rather an opportunity to think about how such differences reflect what actually happens in performance. Every production, on stage or film, cuts, adapts and amends the text to present its own unique version of *Much Ado About Nothing*. This Guide follows the New Cambridge edition of the play (also used in the Cambridge School Shakespeare series).

What did Shakespeare read?

Shakespeare's genius lay in his ability to transform what he read into gripping drama. This section is therefore about the influence of genre: the literary contexts of *Much Ado About Nothing*, which critics today call 'intertextuality' (the way texts influence each other). It identifies the stories and dramatic conventions that fired Shakespeare's imagination as he wrote *Much Ado About Nothing*.

Verse and prose romances (the forerunners of the modern novel) were particularly popular with the Elizabethans, and Shakespeare used many of them for the plots of his plays, particularly in his romantic comedies. These romances were often sentimental in feeling and full of sensational or implausible incidents. They were mainly written in French or Italian, but as they grew in popularity, many were translated into English.

Tales of the slandering of a chaste woman go back to ancient times. It is a theme that has obviously preoccupied societies throughout history. Shakespeare may have got some of his ideas for the Hero–Claudio plot from tales written by the Italian poet Ariosto and the Elizabethan poet Edmund Spenser. In both stories, a lady is accused of being unfaithful and her lover tricked into believing her false by witnessing a servant dressed to look like the lady meeting another man in her bedchamber.

However, Shakespeare's main source for the Hero–Claudio plot was probably from an Italian novella by Matteo Bandello (written in 1554). Bandello's story is set in Messina, Sicily, which is ruled by King Piero of Arragon. The father of Fenecia, the heroine, is Messer Lionato de'Lionati. The following three paragraphs summarise Bandello's story.

Lady Fenecia (i.e. Hero) is falsely accused by Sir Timbreo (i.e. Claudio) after he sees a servant dressed like a gentleman climb a ladder and enter her window. The deception is engineered by Sir Girondo, a friend of Timbreo, who also loves Fenecia. When accused, Fenecia swoons and is apparently dead. When she revives she is sent secretly to the country house of her uncle, where she can assume a different identity. Her funeral, meanwhile, goes ahead.

Within a few days, both Timbreo and Girondo are struck by deep remorse. Girondo confesses to his friend what he has done, asking Timbreo to kill him. But Timbreo forgives his friend and the two confess to Fenecia's father, Lionato. They are both forgiven on condition that Timbreo, when he comes to marry, should take a wife recommended by Lionato.

A year later, after Fenecia has grown to be even more beautiful and scarcely recognisable as the same person, her father Lionato tells Timbreo that he has found a wife for him. Timbreo does not recognise Fenecia and marries her. When, at the wedding breakfast, Timbreo tells with deep grief the story of his mistaken denunciation of Fenecia, the true identity of his new bride is revealed to him.

What is particularly revealing is where Shakespeare departs from his sources, for the departures all tend in the same direction. Shakespeare's lovers (Hero and Claudio) are both made younger, more inexperienced and less inclined (or able) to act independently. Their love is less deep and established. Claudio says virtually nothing to Hero and allows the prince to do his wooing for him. Hero says virtually nothing of her feelings until Claudio is presented to her as a prospective husband, when she had presumably been expecting Don Pedro.

In the Bandello story, Fenecia's father is not wealthy, while Hero's inheritance is uppermost in Claudio's mind. The villain of Shakespeare's story is not, as in Bandello's story, a rival suitor for Hero's love, but a spiteful half-brother to the prince, jealous of the young man's military success. The plot is not disclosed voluntarily by a remorseful perpetrator but is the result of Borachio's drunken boasting.

Timbreo sends a private messenger to Lionato with the accusation of unchastity, while Claudio rejects Hero in a most public and melodramatic way – as Beatrice angrily points out. Unlike Leonato, no one in Fenecia's family believes the accusations of Timbreo. Unlike both Girondo and Timbreo, Claudio shows no sign of remorse at the supposed death of Hero. Remorse only comes when he is proved publicly to have made a false accusation. All these changes suggest that Shakespeare intended Hero to seem virtually defenceless and Claudio to be a particularly callow and unsympathetic young man.

There is no obvious source for the Beatrice–Benedick plot which suggests it is very much Shakespeare's own invention. This is a 'modern' story of a 'modern love' and is strongly contrasted with the Hero–Claudio plot in many ways. However, some slight hints and anticipations of the Beatrice–Benedick story have been found. John Lyly, an older contemporary of Shakespeare, specialised in romance with well-matched lovers speaking elegant prose. Castiglioni's *The Courtier* could also have been a source with its courtly conversation and good-humoured banter between the sexes. In one passage, Castiglione even puts forward the notion that a woman might come to fall in love with a man by hearing it confidently reported that he was in love with her, which has similarities with what happens to Beatrice.

Beatrice is one of a number of Shakespeare's brave, independent, romantic heroines. All of them yield to love in the end, as the comedy genre demands, but not before they have used their shrewd intelligence to battle against male presumptions of superiority.

What was Shakespeare's England like?

Like most writers, ⎮Shakespeare reflected in his plays the world he knew.⎮ His characters in *Much Ado About Nothing* make numerous references to the whole spectrum of Elizabethan town and country life (even in London the countryside was never far away), always with an aptness and imagination which gives life to both character and situation. ⎮

Many aspects of the Elizabethan countryside are alluded to. Claudio believes Don Pedro has wooed Hero for himself, so Benedick compares him to a schoolboy who has had his bird's nest stolen by his best friend. Benedick and Beatrice's friends use hunting and angling terms during their gulling scenes. Claudio likens the unsuspecting Benedick to a dimwitted game bird: 'Oh aye, stalk on, stalk on, the fowl sits' (Act 2 Scene 3, line 83). Hero describes Beatrice scurrying to her hiding place like a lapwing, a bird which looks for prey by running along close to the ground, pausing to look for insects, before running on again (Act 3 Scene 1, lines 24–5). Ursula aptly declares Beatrice to be 'limed' (Act 3 Scene 1, line 104), a reference to catching small birds by coating twigs with sticky bird-lime.

⎮ There are also references to unsavoury city pursuits: gambling, cheating, drinking, casual cruelty and prostitution. If he ever falls in love, Benedick says, they can either hang him up as a sign outside a brothel, or suspend him in a basket like a cat and shoot arrows at him (Act 1 Scene 1, lines 184–92). In a more serious context, Don Pedro talks of his shame at linking his dear friend Claudio 'to a common stale' (Act 4 Scene 1, line 59). Taverns were the favourite haunt of con-men, cheats and gamblers. Dogberry instructs the Watch to check all the alehouses and send the drunks home (Act 3 Scene 3, lines 36–7).

There are two or three casual references in the play which sound racist to modern ears. Benedick says at the end of his gulling scene (Act 2 Scene 3) 'if I do not love her I am a Jew' (i.e. an object of abuse). In Act 3 Scene 4, Margaret wonders if the lovesick Beatrice has not 'turned Turk' (i.e. changed her beliefs radically). Equally disturbing is Claudio's declaration that he will marry Antonio's daughter even if she turns out to be 'an Ethiop' (i.e. dark-skinned). The prejudice in this remark may be as much social as racial. The wealthy leisured classes who could stay indoors saw pale skin as a mark of beauty, while a suntan showed you were one of the poor who worked out of doors. Beatrice says as much when she jokingly imagines ending up as a 'sunburnt' (i.e. unattractive) old spinster (Act 2 Scene 1, lines 241–3).

Elizabethan ideas about health and medical matters are often mentioned. Beatrice says Benedick is a disease more easily 'caught than the pestilence [plague]' (Act 1 Scene 1, line 63). Hero thinks Don John is of a 'melancholy disposition' (Act 2 Scene 1, line 5), a reference to the Elizabethan belief that personality was influenced by four fluids (or humours) in the body. An excess of the melancholy 'humour' rendered a person gloomy and depressed. Some Elizabethans also believed the stars influenced health and personality. Don John knows Conrade was 'born under Saturn' (Act 1 Scene 3, lines 8–9) and therefore expects Conrade to be gloomy like himself.

Elizabethans knew the Bible very well. It was the one book, if any, that they would have had in their homes. They would have appreciated, for example, the ingenious way that Beatrice uses the Scriptures to argue the case for remaining unmarried (Act 2 Scene 1, lines 43–7): since Adam was created out of clay, what woman would want 'to make an account of her life to a clod of wayward marl?' Bombarded with questions from Claudio, Hero desperately cries out 'What kind of catechising call you this?', a reference to the church catechism (a series of questions and answers used to test a believer's faith). The first question in the catechism was 'What is your name?', which prompts Claudio's reply 'To make you answer truly to your name' (Act 4 Scene 1, lines 71–3). Many would also recognise Benedick's reference to 'Don Worm' (Act 5 Scene 2, line 63) as coming from the Book of Isaiah, where a man's conscience is described as a tormenting worm that never dies.

The Elizabethan age was a period of travel and exploration. For example, it was common knowledge to Shakespeare's contemporaries that Sicily had been ruled by Spain for over 300 years. Such knowledge made it easy for audiences to accept that the two highest status characters in *Much Ado About Nothing* are both Spanish, Don Pedro and Don John. But the Elizabethan interest in travel and discovery is perhaps most evident when Benedick tries desperately to avoid Beatrice's company (Act 2 Scene 1, lines 199–205). He asks Don Pedro to send him on an errand as far away as possible: to 'the Antipodes' (opposite side of the world), to 'the furthest inch of Asia' to fetch a toothpick (toothpicks seem to have been an affectation of Elizabethan travellers), to Africa to measure 'the length of Prester John's foot', to the Mongol Empire to get 'a hair off the Great Cham's beard', or to 'the Pygmies' to fetch absolutely *anything*.

The Elizabethan period saw the rise of a new breed of gentlemen, educated and skilled in the administration of the country. This ruling class admired and valued accomplishment in languages, literature and above all public-speaking (rhetoric and oratory). Like the wealthy inhabitants of Messina, they too delighted in showing off their learning. Usually only boys were educated, but girls from wealthy families would also have had tutors. Beatrice, however, rarely makes more than superficial allusions to classical writers – it is not her style – while Benedick seems to enjoy showing off his learning. For example, when he suggests Claudio might be mocking him (Act 1 Scene 1, lines 136–7) he says, 'Or do you play the flouting Jack, to tell us Cupid is a good hare-finder, and Vulcan a rare carpenter?' (Cupid was blind and Vulcan was a blacksmith.) Classical allusions certainly come easily to Benedick. After his bruising encounter with Beatrice in Act 2 Scene 1, he bitterly remarks, 'she would have made Hercules have turned spit, yea, and have cleft his club to make the fire too' (lines 190–2), a reference to Hercules becoming the love-slave of the queen of Lydia (see pages 20, 79–80).

Some references and allusions to Elizabethan life and customs occur insistently, creating particular effects which resonate through the play and question many aspects of Elizabethan society: the place of women, the changing social order, the Elizabethan family, war and politics, honour, excessive ostentation, problems of law and order, attitudes to love and marriage.

The place of women in a patriarchal world

Elizabethan England was in almost every way a patriarchal society. At every point on the social scale men were head of the household. Most decided when and whom their daughters should marry and demanded total respect from their wives and children. A wife was by law subordinate to her husband. She had legal control over neither herself nor her property.

This patriarchal attitude underlies much of Leonato and Antonio's behaviour in the play. Antonio says to Hero, 'Well, niece, I trust you will be ruled by your father' (Act 2 Scene 1, line 38), whereupon Leonato reminds her (lines 48–9) how to behave should the prince come to woo her; yet when it transpires that the prince woos on behalf of Claudio not himself, Leonato has no qualms about the sudden change of son-in-law.

For the wealthy Elizabethan classes, a bride had above all to be a virgin to avoid future disputes over inheritance, and many in Shakespeare's audience would have understood how that fear might provoke the denunciation of Hero in Act 4 Scene 1. Few would have questioned Leonato's giving of Hero in marriage to Claudio a second time. It was a father's legal right to do so.

Hero does her best to play the dutiful and obedient daughter, although her silence makes it difficult to surmise what she might be thinking. Her comments about Beatrice in Act 3 Scene 1, however, suggest a certain envy and resentment at her cousin's more liberated behaviour, and her tetchy outburst in Act 3 Scene 4 ('My cousin's a fool and thou art another') strikes a brief spark of individuality. Yet even so, many modern audiences and actors find her behaviour hard to take. One late twentieth-century actress playing Hero commented that, instead of fainting, she would have replied to Claudio something like: 'If you won't take my word for my innocence, then as far as I'm concerned the marriage is off.'

Elizabethan men also drew on a variety of stereotyped views about women, all of which are echoed by male characters at various points in the play:

- Women are by nature promiscuous. Hence all the cuckolding jokes and Benedick's deep suspicion of marriage. A woman's greatest virtue was chastity. Without that she was worthless, as Claudio makes abundantly clear in Act 4 Scene 1.
- Women are created by God solely for marriage and childbearing. Even Beatrice, when she watches Hero's betrothal, feels a certain regret that she may end up an old maid.
- Women are goddesses to be worshipped and adored. This 'courtly love' approach is a more subtle strategy which appears to show respect and love for a woman. Yet, as one critic remarked: 'To see a woman as a goddess is to silence her as a human being.' Claudio speaks of Hero in adoring terms in both Act 1 Scene 1 and Act 4 Scene 1. But he never really talks with her.
- Women are shrews and scolds. Women could by law be punished for talking too much. Women who showed intelligence and independence were 'curst', an accusation which both Antonio and Leonato level at Beatrice in Act 2 Scene 1.
- Women are scapegoats. Eve tempted Adam, so that mankind was banished from Paradise. Women were therefore responsible for all the ills of the world. Beatrice, Hero and Ursula are all on the receiving end of male criticism at some point in the play.

Yet in some quarters of Elizabethan society, this repressive attitude to women was being seriously questioned. There were talented and liberated women at Elizabeth's court (besides the queen herself) who had already fought and won the battle for a greater degree of equality, women whom Shakespeare may have used as a model for Beatrice. Some Puritans asserted a spiritual equality and companionship between men and women and pressed for the granting of women's rights and reform of the inhumane marriage customs. Similar attitudes were to be found among the families of merchants and wealthy artisans, as well as the gentry, many of whom (both men and women) would have made up Shakespeare's audience.

Beatrice is indeed strikingly independent. It is she who questions Leonato and Antonio's assumption of a father's rights over his daughter (Act 2 Scene 1, lines 39–41); she who from her first words undermines and ridicules the male posturing in the play ('I pray you, is Signor Mountanto returned from the wars or no?'); who first denounces the behaviour of the prince and Count Claudio in Act 4

Scene 1, lines 301–7 ('Princes and counties!'); who most effectively defends Hero, raging both at her own weakness and the weakness of men.

Shakespeare may have seen men and women as equals and also realised that they lived in a very unequal world, yet for all his sympathetic insight into a world where men had all the power and made the rules, he refrains from openly advocating radical reform in the social status of women. In an Elizabethan comedy, the main characters have to marry: that was what the genre demanded and the audience expected. *Much Ado About Nothing* therefore appears to say that for women, even ones like Hero and Beatrice, marriage is realistically the only option. There would probably have been few people in Shakespeare's day who would have seriously disagreed.

The Elizabethan social order

Elizabethan England was a society in a state of transition. The old feudal world, where people were expected to show unquestioning loyalty and respect for those of superior rank, was giving way to a new more socially mobile society driven by commerce, new industries and personal enterprise. Many of the increasingly prosperous merchant and landowning classes were pushing themselves up into the ranks of the aristocracy through marriage, rather as Leonato's family does. This tension between the old order and the new is very much reflected in the play, for, despite their Italian or Spanish titles, Leonato and his guests closely resemble the nobility and the wealthy merchant classes of Shakespeare's day.

The traditional feudal deference is clearly signalled in the opening scene. Governor Leonato has no title but is clearly wealthy. He could be a successful Elizabethan merchant or gentleman landowner, appointed to high public office. His main guests, however, are of much higher rank. Don Pedro, prince of Arragon, is respectfully addressed as 'your grace', 'my lord' and 'your highness'. Claudio is a count (the equivalent of an English earl) and of higher rank than his friend Benedick, even though Don Pedro addresses them both as 'Signor'. Despite the warmth and friendship between them, everyone observes these distinctions of rank in the early scenes.

This social respect, however, is seriously undermined in the course of the play by Don John's slandering of Hero's good name. Leonato at first believes the charge against Hero simply because his superiors have said so: 'Would the two princes lie, and Claudio lie'? (Act 4 Scene 1, line 145). Beatrice, as always, is the first to question her superiors' authority and the sarcasm in her words is all too clear: 'Princes and counties! Surely a princely testimony, a goodly count, Count Comfect, a sweet gallant surely' (Act 4 Scene 1, lines 301-2). Initially, only Beatrice and the Friar believe Hero's story but their conviction wins over first Benedick, then Leonato and Antonio, until all three in turn challenge Claudio, addressing him in the most insulting manner, calling him 'Sir Boy' and 'Lord Lack-beard'.

With the discovery of Don John's plot, the play ends in apparent harmony, but the audience is left with an uncomfortable vision of a society where respect is not earned through individual merit, but merely inherited. Despite the noble Claudio's unforgivable behaviour, his penance is brief, Leonato's anger even briefer and Hero is offered for a second time as a reward to the very man who had so cruelly and publicly shamed her.

War, politics and male honour

Struggles for power between members of the same royal family were not unusual in Shakespeare's time. A bastard offspring like Don John was a particular threat, because he threatened to challenge the claims of a legitimate heir like Don Pedro. Bastards were therefore regarded as evil and malicious and frequently appeared in the theatre as the stage villain. Elizabeth I herself was regarded by her enemies as the bastard daughter of Henry VIII and there were many plots to replace her with her cousin, Mary Queen of Scots. Elizabeth's court was also full of ambitious and potentially rebellious lords, to whom Hero perhaps refers when she describes the honeysuckle in the arbour growing so luxuriantly in the sun and shutting out the light 'like favourites, / Made proud by princes, that advance their pride, / Against that power that bred it' (Act 3 Scene 1, lines 9-11). Elizabeth's favourite, the Earl of Essex, led one such rebellion in 1601, not long after the play was written. That the play begins with news of the conclusion of a military campaign, comes to a crisis with challenges to single combat and ends with the uneasy possibility that a new war might soon break out, would have seemed perfectly credible to an Elizabethan audience.

Every Elizabethan male was expected to fight for his country if needed. Those wealthy enough were obliged to equip themselves with horses, arms and armour. Sunday practice with the longbow at the archery butts was also obligatory despite the development of firearms (hence Benedick's comment about Beatrice's wit: 'I stood like a man at a mark, with a whole army shooting at me' Act 2 Scene 1, lines 186–7). The play is full of references to swords and bucklers, pikes, scabbards, lances, poniards (daggers) and it is not only the male characters who use them. Beatrice frequently uses the men's own military language against them in her criticism of male values (see pages 77–8).

Close bonds of male friendship, especially those forged in war, were very much valued in Elizabethan times, and the three comrades speak to each other with the typical male banter of friendly abuse. Some critics have argued that distrust of women is the basis of all-male bonds. As is clear from Act 1 Scene 1, Benedick certainly has adopted such a misogynistic pose at the start of the play.

Don John's plot quickly brings to the surface a darker side to this masculine military world. Cuckolding jokes about other men's wives are fine, but the wife of an Elizabethan noble must be above suspicion. Hero's perceived infidelity has shamed Claudio in the eyes of his comrades and must be publicly avenged. When he denounces Hero (Act 4 Scene 1), virtually all the men assume she is guilty simply because her accusers are men of honour. Even the Friar accepts that Hero's 'wounded reputation' may require her removal from society.

This masculine value code is eventually challenged by Benedick, persuaded by his love for Beatrice to risk death for Hero. Although the crisis is resolved without bloodshed, the experience clearly changes Benedick. His love for Beatrice has moved him onto a new level of seeing and feeling. His military friends, however, remain firmly in their old male world, cracking their tired cuckolding jokes to the very end.

The Elizabethan household

Aristocrats lived vastly different lives from the average Elizabethan citizen, having both time and money for eating, relaxation and entertainment. The play contains, for example, frequent references to food, dinners, banquets and great suppers. Don John does not go to the main meal, (the 'great supper'), but does attend the dancing afterwards and then follows the other guests to the 'banquet', which was a light dessert/ sweetmeat course that often followed an elaborate meal. The food at these banquets was often strikingly presented in exotically shaped vessels (Benedick talks about Claudio's words turning into a 'fantastical banquet, just so many strange dishes' Act 2 Scene 3, line 17).

The increasingly wealthy gentry and merchant classes built new houses in great numbers and there was rivalry as to who owned the richest and most fashionable house. It was an honour to have, like Leonato, a dwelling grand enough for a queen or prince to stay in. Most of the household's affairs would take place in the Great Hall, which was where the household dined, entertainments like dances took place and the master of the house conducted his business.

Wealthy Elizabethans also took pride in their orchards and gardens and, like the characters in the play, loved to relax there. Oranges and lemons were first brought back to England in the Middle Ages by the Crusaders, but were still relatively rare and exotic in Elizabethan England. A symbol of wealth and luxury, they were sometimes grown in pots or under glass in orangeries. Beatrice observes that the unhappy Claudio is as 'civil as an orange, and something of that jealous complexion' (Act 2 Scene 1, lines 223–4). The Seville orange (also spelt 'civil') was a sharp-tasting yellow fruit used for flavouring food and making marmalade. Claudio in his turn echoes her words at the church when he refers bitterly to Hero as 'this rotten orange' (Act 4 Scene 1, line 27).

There was very little privacy in a wealthy Elizabethan house, even one as grand as Leonato's, because an Elizabethan household was quite extensive. First there was the immediate family, then other relations (like Beatrice), waiting gentlewomen (like Ursula and Margaret), servants, workers on the estate, and so on. During the day, a lady's bedchamber could have as many as 20 people working there. At night Hero did not even sleep alone (Act 4 Scene 1, lines 141–2). It is no surprise, therefore, that a favourite pastime of almost everyone in the play is gossip and eavesdropping.

An age of ostentation

Elizabethans liked to display their wealth, especially in the way they dressed. An Elizabethan aristocrat, taking his or her cue from the queen, was a rich and glittering sight. In the late sixteenth century, costumes for both sexes became extremely ornate and vastly expensive as both men and women strove to outshine their rivals. In Act 3 Scene

4, Margaret describes in sumptuous detail the Duchess of Milan's wedding gown (lines 14–18). Since Elizabethan theatre companies often possessed an impressive array of rich costumes (some purchased second-hand from the nobility and gentry), it would have been easy for them to recreate on stage something of that fashionable splendour.

In the eyes of the traditionalists, men's fashions had become particularly effeminate and extravagant by the end of the sixteenth century. Some noblemen wore make-up, had their hair curled at the barber's, wore single earrings and smothered themselves in perfume, very like Benedick does in Act 3 Scene 2, to the amusement of his friends. Moralists of the day were particularly incensed by the lovelock, a long strand of hair grown down over one shoulder, which one of the watchmen remembers the imaginary Deformed sporting.

The fashionable English gallant, who might copy any foreign style that took his fancy, mixing them in the most outrageous way, was a favourite subject of ridicule with Elizabethan writers. Foreigners often commented on how frequently the English changed their fashions, particularly their hats, a fact which provides ammunition for Beatrice to fire at Benedick (Act 1 Scene 1, lines 55–6).

Shakespeare, however, uses the fashions of the time for more than mere ridicule, such as when Antonio calls Claudio a 'fashion-monging' boy (Act 5 Scene 1, line 93). At crucial moments in the plot to dishonour Hero, fashion references become much more insistent. When Borachio broaches the plan to Don John, he says he 'will so fashion the matter, that Hero shall be absent' on the crucial night. Then, when the deception has been successful, he talks with Conrade cynically and at length about that 'deformed thief' fashion (Act 3 Scene 3, lines 96–117). When brought before Don Pedro, he speaks of how the prince and Claudio saw him 'court Margaret in Hero's garments' (Act 5 Scene 1, line 209), a fact which has not been mentioned before in the play. It is as if the elaborate and fantastic fashions of the day, with all their padding and deforming of the human shape, have come to symbolise the gulf between appearance and reality which is so much a preoccupation of the play. It is ironic that such a shrewd observation should be given to the unscrupulous Borachio.

Law and order

Justices of the Peace, parish constables and the Town Watch were virtually the sole guardians of law and order in Shakespeare's time.

There was no professional police force as we know it. Petty lawlessness and violence had risen inexorably during Elizabeth's reign, reaching a peak at about the time the play was written. The rich may have grown richer during Elizabeth I's reign, but the poor had become dramatically poorer. Increasing numbers of landless, starving vagrants and beggars turned in desperation to crime, terrorising the towns and countryside. If Leonato had carried out his wish to adopt 'a beggar's issue' (Act 4 Scene 1, line 125) in place of Hero, he would have had plenty to choose from. Ever harsher punishments were meted out by the authorities and record numbers were sent to the gallows in a vain attempt to stem the tide of crime. Characters in the play sometimes make joking references to these savage punishments: hanging, drawing, quartering (Act 3 Scene 2, lines 16–19) and burning at the stake (Act 1 Scene 1, lines 172–3); or make more serious references: torturing to death (Act 4 Scene 1, line 177) and crushing with weights (Act 5 Scene 1, line 244).

The Justices conducted the trial and punishment of less important criminals. They were customarily selected from the local gentry. Leonato acts very much like an English Justice of the Peace in his dealings with Dogberry. Justices were unpaid and had to cope with an increasing number of cases in their spare time. Many must have found their public duties constantly interrupting their private life, as Leonato does on his daughter's wedding day. One early twentieth-century production showed Leonato on the morning of the wedding dealing with last-minute business papers as he talked to Dogberry and Verges.

The constables were also unpaid local men elected to the job for one year. Few wanted to take up such a thankless public duty and often paid some poor man to do the job for them, which is perhaps how Dogberry and Verges came to be appointed. Many constables were either too old or incompetent to stop fights or arrest thieves and few people had any respect for them. It was not unusual for a constable to seek to avoid trouble wherever possible, as Dogberry advises the Watch to do in Act 3 Scene 3. The following comment from a seventeenth-century writer could almost be describing Dogberry:

> I have known by my own experience that when hue and cry
> have been made even to the faces of some constables, they have
> said 'God restore your loss! I have other business at this time.'

In the towns, nightwatchmen (the Watch) were employed to help the constable. These too were often old, lazy or incompetent. They were armed only with a pole or pike, a lantern and sometimes a bell to summon help. Their duties were to patrol the streets from dusk to dawn looking out for wrongdoers and questioning anyone they found wandering about. Like the constables, they often shirked their duties, eager only to avoid trouble.

> We will rather sleep than talk, we know what belongs to a
> watch.   *(Act 3 Scene 3, lines 32–3)*

Dogberry and the Watch are quintessentially English. Tradition has it that Shakespeare modelled Dogberry on a real constable who lived at Grendon in Buckinghamshire, which he would have passed through on his way from Stratford-upon-Avon to London.

Attitudes to love and marriage in Elizabethan England

Marriages amongst the Elizabethan gentry were traditionally a means of providing heirs to secure the family name and property. A man would look to marry a woman of his own social level, or from a class beneath him if her family was wealthy enough (rather as Claudio marries Hero). Although mutual esteem, affection, companionship could all develop within a marriage, Elizabethans did not necessarily believe them to be prerequisites. Indeed, love (in the sense of sexual desire) as a reason for marrying was constantly attacked by some moralists of the day.

Yet the fact that Shakespeare (in this and other comedies) explores in great detail the nature of love and marriage suggests that attitudes were changing. To put it perhaps over-simply, the play's Hero–Claudio plot shows the conventional rituals of an aristocratic wooing and wedding, while the Beatrice–Benedick plot presents newer thinking on what the relationship between love and marriage might be.

It is easy to be persuaded by Claudio's poetic language that he truly loves Hero, but in the play he never speaks to her before the betrothal. It is solely her outward beauty and charm (plus of course her inheritance) which wins his heart. What he and Don Pedro call 'love' is merely playing the role of the courtly lover, a way of sugaring over what is essentially a business transaction. First there is the proxy wooing and dowry settlement (all haggling conducted tactfully offstage), then the formal betrothal and marriage – everything over in just seven days. Benedick is deeply unimpressed (Act 2 Scene 3, lines 7–17). Claudio, newly transformed into Elizabethan lover, he says, now lies awake thinking about fashionable doublets, talks in an elaborate flowery language and delights in love music. Don Pedro arranges for a serenade to Hero at her window. Hero is sent perfumed gloves, a traditional Elizabethan courting gift. It is courtship 'by numbers', ritualistic and ceremonial. There is no 'getting to know you', no meeting of minds. It is all very much as Beatrice perceptively describes it in Act 2 Scene 1 (lines 52–7) – a series of pre-set dances that all must follow.

Surprisingly, even the sceptical Beatrice and Benedick take on conventional male and female roles when they 'fall in love'. Benedick claims it is his duty to procreate ('The world must be peopled'), while Beatrice promises like a dutiful wife to tame her 'wild heart' to Benedick's 'loving hand'. Benedick even outshines his friend Claudio in the externalities of the courtly lover role. He shaves off his beard, gets toothache (love and illness, especially toothache, traditionally went together), puts on perfume and make-up, wears outrageously fashionable clothes, sings love songs (pitifully) and writes 'halting' sonnets (badly). Beatrice is more restrained, but even she falls ill (with a cold) and pens a love sonnet.

The heart of the play, however, lies in the fact that Beatrice and Benedick's love is so much more than mere superficiality. In them, Shakespeare presents two prickly, unconventional people coming to terms with the traditional social roles expected of them, a destiny which, by posing as 'scorners of love', they have so far managed to resist.

Language

Contrary to the popular belief that he was a 'natural' writer, utterly spontaneous, inspired only by his imagination, Shakespeare had a profound knowledge of the language techniques of his own and previous times. Behind the apparent effortlessness of his writing lies a deeply practised skill, which is very much evident in the flexible and varied language of *Much Ado About Nothing*. The play displays a wide variety of language registers: blank verse, rhyming couplets, quatrains, lyrical songs, and prose that is by turns heavily patterned, elegantly balanced, witty and combative, angry and abusive, precariously rambling. Furthermore, the wordplay, especially puns, in *Much Ado About Nothing* is a way of alerting the audience to the fact that the play is concerned with the ambiguity of language, how people can so easily mistake meaning.

What follows is a brief analysis of some of the language techniques Shakespeare uses in *Much Ado About Nothing* to intensify dramatic effect, create mood and character, and so produce memorable theatre. The techniques are found in verse and prose alike. As you read the play, always keep in mind the fact that Shakespeare wrote for theatre-goers, not readers. He wrote lines for actors to speak, which had to be understood as soon as they were heard, in a crowded open-air theatre. Elizabethan dramatic language, because written to be heard, tends to be more patterned, with distinctive rhythms and repetitions of words and phrases to help the audience keep track of what the actor is saying. Actors will, in addition, seek to use a range of verbal and non-verbal methods to exploit the dramatic possibilities of the language: voice, facial expressions, gestures and actions.

Imagery

Much Ado About Nothing abounds in imagery (sometimes called 'figurative language'): vivid words and phrases that help create the atmosphere of the play as they conjure up emotionally-charged pictures in the imagination. Beatrice, for example, frequently uses imagery to undermine the male military values in the play: Benedick is 'Signor Mountanto' ('mountanto' = a fancy fencing term), he has no 'stomach' (courage), their every meeting is a 'conflict' where she is 'boarded' and his insulting comparisons are 'broken' on her like clumsily wielded lances.

At times Shakespeare uses imagery, rather as a modern director uses lighting and setting, to create particular atmospheric effects. For example, Hero's image of 'the pleachèd bower' with its 'honeysuckles ripened by the sun', or Don Pedro's description at the end of the funeral scene of how 'gentle day / . . . / Dapples the drowsy east with spots of grey'. Indeed, Shakespeare seems to have thought in images, and the whole play richly demonstrates his unflagging and varied use of verbal illustration, right from the twelfth line of the play when the Messenger describes Claudio's battle heroics as 'doing in the figure of a lamb the feats of a lion'.

Early critics, such as John Dryden and Doctor Johnson, were critical of Shakespeare's fondness for imagery. They felt that many images obscured meaning and detracted attention from the subjects they represented. Over the past two hundred years, however, critics, poets and audiences have increasingly valued Shakespeare's imagery. They recognise how he uses it to give pleasure as it stirs the audience's imagination, deepens the dramatic impact of particular moments or moods, provides insight into character, and intensifies meaning and emotional force. Images carry powerful significance far deeper than their surface meanings.

As the Contexts section shows, Shakespeare's Elizabethan world provides much of the play's imagery. Benedick laments that the lovestruck Claudio has exchanged the military drum and fife for the lover's tabor and pipe; Borachio compares the young Elizabethan 'hot-bloods' to figures on church wall paintings, stained glass windows and moth-eaten tapestries: 'like Pharaoh's soldiers in the reechy painting, sometime like god Bel's priests in the old church window, sometime like the shaven Hercules in the smirched worm-eaten tapestry'.

Shakespeare's imagery uses metaphor, simile and personification. All are comparisons which in effect substitute one thing (the image) for another (the thing described).

- A simile compares one thing to another using 'like' or 'as'. Benedick thinks that Beatrice would exceed Hero 'as much in beauty as the first of May doth the last of December' if only she didn't have such a terrible temper. Don Pedro, on hearing Borachio confirm Hero's innocence, asks Claudio, 'Runs not this speech like iron through your blood?'

- A metaphor is also a comparison. It does not use 'like' or 'as', but suggests that two dissimilar things are actually the same. Leonato expresses his anger and disgust at his daughter's presumed immorality in a sequence of three powerful metaphors (staining, cleansing and corruption):

> why she, oh she is fallen
> Into a pit of ink, that the wide sea
> Hath drops too few to wash her clean again,
> And salt too little, which may season give
> To her foul tainted flesh.   *(Act 4 Scene 1, lines 132–6)*

At crucial moments, an image will echo key themes in the play, such as knowing appearance from reality. When Claudio returns Hero to her father with the words 'Give not this rotten orange to your friend', he powerfully evokes a sense of outer beauty and inner corruption.

- Personification turns all kinds of things into persons, giving them human feelings or attributes. Beatrice talks of 'Repentance, . . . with his bad legs'; Dogberry brings in the captured Borachio with the words 'Come you, sir, if justice cannot tame you, she shall ne'er weigh more reasons in her balance'.

Classical mythology also contributes to the richness of the play's imagery (Elizabethans were generally more familiar with such figures than most members of a modern audience). There are numerous references to figures in classical mythology: Cupid and Venus (deities of love), Diana (goddess of chastity), Hymen (goddess of marriage) and Ate (goddess of discord); Jove, Phoebus Apollo, Vulcan, Hercules; Hector, Troilus, Leander, Europa and the Harpies.

Characters sometimes use classical allusions to impress. At the masked dance, Don Pedro hints to Hero that a handsome face lies hidden behind his visor (mask), likening himself to the god Jove visiting Philemon's humble cottage: 'My visor is Philemon's roof, within the house is Jove' (Act 2 Scene 1, line 69); to which Hero wittily replies, perhaps referring to Don Pedro's bald head, 'Why then your visor should be thatched.'

Sometimes the classical allusions have a sharper bite to them. After his painful encounter with Beatrice, Benedick claims she would have humiliated Hercules (see page 66), and compares her to Ate, the goddess of discord, who lived by the gates of hell (see below).

Many of these classical allusions also echo preoccupations in the play, such as infidelity in love and the emasculation of man by woman. Claudio compares the lovestruck Benedick to the god Jove, who seduced Europa in the form of a bull. Jove, king of the gods, was a serial adulterer. To keep his sexual liaisons secret from his wife, he adopted many disguises (e.g. bull, satyr, swan) when he seduced young mortal women like Europa.

All the types of imagery so far mentioned (simile, metaphor, personification and classical allusion) are used one after another during Benedick's account of his traumatic masked dance with Beatrice (Act 2 Scene 1, lines 181–97). Even his own visor came to life and joined Beatrice in mocking him (personification); her words were stabbing 'poniards' (metaphor); he was defenceless 'like a man at a mark, with a whole army shooting at me' (simile); in his eyes, Beatrice is 'the infernal Ate in good apparel' (classical allusion).

Antithesis

Antithesis is the opposition of words or phrases against each other, as when Beatrice exclaims, 'I had rather hear my dog bark at a crow than a man swear he loves me' (Act 1 Scene 1, lines 97–8). This setting of a word/phrase/image against another (e.g. 'dog bark' stands in contrast to 'man swear') is one of Shakespeare's favourite language devices. He uses it extensively in all his plays, because antithesis powerfully expresses conflict through its use of opposites, and conflict is the essence of all drama.

Shakespeare's dramatic style is characterised by his concern for comparison and contrast, opposition and juxtaposition: he sets character against character, scene against scene, emotional tone against emotional tone, word against word, phrase against phrase. Indeed, *Much Ado About Nothing* is very much a play of 'doubles' where antitheses and juxtapositions occur in many forms: the 'merry war' between Beatrice and Benedick; the contrasting traditional courtship of Hero by Claudio; the rivalry of the brothers Don Pedro and Don John; Leonato's manipulation of the dutiful Hero and Beatrice's liberated resistance to all forms of male dominance. Through antithesis, Shakespeare can even reveal something of a character's inner life, as when Leonato says of his niece, 'she hath often dreamed of unhappiness, and waked herself with laughing' (Act 2 Scene 1, lines 261–2).

In the play as a whole, however, there is a deeper antithesis, a persistent sense that things are not as they seem, a dissonance between appearance and reality. The punning on 'nothing' and 'noting' in the title (see pages 4, 115, 117) suggests from the start that the play is concerned with perception. Characters are continually faced with the question: 'Can I be certain that what I see, or hear, or know is true?' This uncertainty escalates quickly through a complex series of mistakings and deceptions into the near-tragic belief in the 'truth' of Hero's unfaithfulness. Claudio's farewell to Hero is full of antitheses:

> But fare thee well, most foul, most fair, farewell
> Thou pure impiety, and impious purity
>
> *(Act 4 Scene 1, lines 96–7)*

Repetition

Different forms of language repetition run through the play, contributing to its atmosphere, creation of character and dramatic force. Apart from familiar functional words ('the', 'and', etc.) one of the lexical words most frequently repeated is 'love' (used 90 times). Its repetition is a clear indication of the major preoccupation of the play. (See also pages 92, 115.)

Repeated words, phrases, rhythms and sounds add intensity to the moment or episode. They can heighten theatrical effect and deepen emotional and imaginative significance. At first in the play, repetitions, like antitheses, are used elegantly and playfully. Benedick jokes with his friends about troths and faiths:

DON PEDRO By my troth, I speak my thought.
CLAUDIO And in faith, my lord, I spoke mine.
BENEDICK And by my two faiths and troths, my lord, I spoke mine.

> *(Act 1 Scene 1, lines 166–8)*

This is all in sharp contrast with, for example, the intensity of Leonato's later outburst of shame and disappointment, with its repeated questions and repetitions of 'I' and 'one':

> Grieved I, I had but one?
> Chid I for that at frugal nature's frame?
> Oh one too much by thee! Why had I one?
> Why ever wast thou lovely in my eyes?
>
> *(Act 4 Scene 1, lines 120–3)*

Like antithesis, repetition can also suggest distinctive features of a character's personality. One of the most obvious examples of this is Dogberry, whose obsessive repetition of words and phrases is evidence of his 'tediousness':

> I am a wise fellow, and which is more, an officer, and which is more, a householder, and which is more, as pretty a piece of flesh as any is in Messina, and one that knows the law, go to, and a rich fellow enough, go to, and a fellow that hath losses, and one that hath two gowns, and everything handsome about him: bring him away: oh that I had been writ down an ass!
>
> *(Act 4 Scene 2, lines 65–71)*

Perhaps most significantly, repetition helps to embody Benedick and Beatrice's bickering relationship. At their first encounter they take up each other's words only to hurl back a new insult ('Lady Disdain . . . Disdain . . . Courtesy . . . Courtesy . . . scratched . . . Scratching . . . parrot-teacher . . . bird . . . beast . . . horse . . . jade's trick'). These quick-witted ripostes, however, become intensely earnest repetitions in the church, as they pick up on words like 'friends' and 'enemy':

BEATRICE In faith I will go.

BENEDICK We'll be friends first.

BEATRICE You dare easier be friends with me, than fight with mine enemy.

BENEDICK Is Claudio thine enemy?   *(Act 4 Scene 1, lines 286–90)*

Even their final admission of love is a battle of repeated phrases and rhythms: 'by this light I take thee for pity', says Benedick; 'by this good day, I yield upon great persuasion', replies Beatrice.

Lists

One of Shakespeare's favourite language methods is to accumulate words or phrases rather like a list, intensifying and varying description, atmosphere and argument as he 'piles up' item on item, incident on incident. Every list in *Much Ado About Nothing* has its dramatic purposes.

Sometimes a list comprises only single words or phrases, such as Claudio's gloriously over-the-top description of Beatrice's lovestricken 'grief' (Act 2 Scene 3, lines 126–8): 'Then down upon her knees she falls, weeps, sobs, beats her heart, tears her hair, prays, curses, Oh sweet Benedick, God give me patience.' Other lists are brief descriptions, such as Hero's listing of the many kinds of men Beatrice would 'spell backwards' (Act 3 Scene 1, lines 59–67), or Don Pedro's description of Benedick's geographically eclectic sense of fashion (Act 3 Scene 2, lines 24–8). Yet other lists are used to abuse: for example, Benedick's list of all the faraway places he is willing to be sent to in order to avoid 'this Harpy' (Act 2 Scene 1, lines 199–205).

Some lists help to develop character portrayal, such as Don John's brooding account of his personal qualities: 'I cannot hide what I am . . .' (Act 1 Scene 3, lines 10–13). Benedick, just before he is gulled into loving Beatrice, complacently lists all the women he is immune to: 'one woman is fair, yet I am well: another is wise, yet I am well . . .', then lists all the demanding qualities his ideal woman must possess, climaxing with the generous concession that 'her hair shall be of what colour it please God' (Act 2 Scene 3, lines 21–7). He later speaks the most loving and anticlimactic list when declaring how much he loves Beatrice:

BEATRICE Will you go hear this news, signor?
BENEDICK I will live in thy heart, die in thy lap, and be buried in thy eyes: and moreover, I will go with thee to thy uncle's.

(Act 5 Scene 2, lines 77–9)

Malapropisms

Dogberry's particular talent is for malapropisms (mistakenly using one word for another similar word). The term derives from Mrs Malaprop, a character in Sheridan's late eighteenth-century play, *The Rivals*, who misapplied words very much like Dogberry. There is a significant difference, however. While Mrs Malaprop amusingly confuses similar sounding words ('He is the very pineapple of politeness'; 'as headstrong as an allegory on the banks of the Nile'), Dogberry often confuses similar sounding words *antithetically* (i.e.

with words of opposite meaning). So a deserving man becomes a 'desartless man', a sensible and fit man becomes a 'senseless and fit man' and Verges' once sharp wits 'are not so blunt, as . . . they were'.

This inversion of meanings very much reflects Dogberry's general approach to life, law enforcement and criminals. He believes sleeping on duty is good because it helps keep the streets peaceful and advises decent virtuous men like the Watch to have as little to do as possible with vagrants, rowdy drunks or thieves (Act 3 Scene 3, lines 21–60). Dogberry's antithetical malapropisms also illustrate once again the play's concern with distinguishing reality from appearance. Where others in the play deliberately use language to distort and deceive, Dogberry baffles by unwittingly 'reversing' language.

Verse and prose

An Elizabethan audience would have been more sensitively attuned than a modern audience to the difference between verse and prose spoken on stage and would have responded differently to each. They expected the high-status characters to speak verse, particularly in 'serious' scenes where the more stylised language of verse was thought particularly suitable for lovers and for scenes of high drama or emotional intensity. Prose was the traditional vehicle for comedy and was typically spoken by the low-status characters in the more 'relaxed' comic scenes. More than two-thirds of *Much Ado About Nothing* is in prose.

Dogberry, unequivocally a comic character, always speaks in prose, but elsewhere Shakespeare switches from verse to prose in subtly dramatic ways. High-status characters, like Leonato, Claudio and Don Pedro, speak an elegant prose when relaxed, yet when the situation becomes more serious they use verse. Claudio, for example, leads Don Pedro into verse to talk of his love for Hero (Act 1 Scene 1). When Benedick's friends begin their gulling (Act 2 Scene 3), they first soften him up with romantic verse talk, while the hidden Benedick stubbornly delivers his asides in prose. Then, after Balthasar's song, his friends also switch to prose as they pretend to relax and discuss Beatrice's problems in love.

Shakespeare also switches between prose and verse as part of the dramatic construction of entire scenes. The Benedick gulling scene (predominantly in prose) is usually played more humorously than the

Beatrice scene (entirely in verse), which is played more 'feelingly'. The use of verse and prose in the wedding scene (Act 4 Scene 1) helps to balance and contrast the two crisis points in the Hero–Claudio and Beatrice–Benedick plots. Although the audience is aware that Claudio and Don Pedro believe Hero is unfaithful, the scene begins, seemingly pleasantly, in prose, until Claudio switches to verse to denounce Hero. The scene continues in verse (for 230 lines), but switches back to prose when Beatrice and Benedick are left alone together on stage. Perhaps Shakespeare felt the power and formality of verse was appropriate for Claudio and Leonato's anger, disgust and disappointment, while the more 'natural' rhythms of prose were more appropriate for Beatrice and Benedick's discovery of their love for each other.

Some characters seem to be given a preferred medium for speaking in. Beatrice and Benedick instinctively speak in prose, as befits their rational and worldly wise outlook on life and love. However, they do sometimes speak in verse at dramatically intense moments. Overcome with emotion at hearing of Benedick's love for her (Act 3 Scene 1), Beatrice speaks for the first time in verse. She uses not just blank verse but rhyming verse in abbreviated sonnet form (two quatrains and a final couplet):

> What fire is in mine ears? Can this be true?
> Stand I condemned for pride and scorn so much?
> Contempt, farewell, and maiden pride, adieu,
> No glory lies behind the back of such.
> And Benedick, love on, I will requite thee,
> Taming my wild heart to thy loving hand:
> If thou dost love, my kindness shall incite thee
> To bind our loves up in a holy band,
> For others say thou dost deserve, and I
> Believe it better than reportingly.   *(lines 107–16)*

Although less formally or obviously patterned than his verse, Shakespeare's prose is nonetheless carefully structured, possessing in looser form the same linguistic features as are found in his verse: imagery, rhythms, repetitions, antitheses and lists. Within his prose speeches and dialogue, the sentences, phrases and words frequently balance, reflect or oppose each other. Many of these features can be seen in Beatrice and Leonato's conversation at the start of Act 2 Scene

1, where the resulting effect is a powerful sense of shared fun and playing with ideas:

BEATRICE He were an excellent man that were made just in the mid-
            way between him [Don John] and Benedick: the one is too like
            an image and says nothing, and the other too like my lady's
            eldest son, evermore tattling.
LEONATO Then half Signor Benedick's tongue in Count John's
            mouth, and half Count John's melancholy in Signor Benedick's
            face –
BEATRICE With a good leg and a good foot, uncle, and money
            enough in his purse, such a man would win any woman in the
            world if a could get her good will.   *(lines 6–13)*

Although only one-third of the play is written in blank verse, it is spoken at significant moments and with powerful effect. Blank verse (unrhymed verse written in iambic pentameter) is the standard verse form for all of Shakespeare's plays. In Greek, *penta* means 'five' and *iamb* means a 'foot' of two syllables, the first unstressed and the second stressed, as in 'My liege' = My LIEGE. Iambic pentameter is therefore a metre in which each line has five alternating unstressed (×) and stressed (/) syllables, as in the first verse line of the play:

     × /   × / × /   × / × /
     My liege, your highness now may do me good.
                                        (Act 1 Scene 1, line 216)

Shakespeare's early plays, such as *Titus Andronicus* or *Richard III*, have a very regular rhythm (often expressed as de-DUM, de-DUM, de-DUM, de-DUM, de-DUM), with 'end-stopping' (sense-pauses at the end of each line). By the time he came to write *Much Ado About Nothing* (*c.* 1598), Shakespeare had become more flexible and experimental in his use of iambic pentameter. The 'five-beat' metre is still present but less prominent, more like a background rhythm. There are fewer end-stopped lines, more mid-line sense-pauses (*caesuras*) and more run-on lines (*enjambement*), where the sense of one line flows on into the next, seemingly with little or no pause, as in Antonio and Leonato's opening words in Act 5:

ANTONIO If you go on thus, you will kill yourself,
       And 'tis not wisdom thus to second grief,
       Against yourself.
LEONATO   I pray thee cease thy counsel,
       Which falls into mine ears as profitless,
       As water in a sieve   *(Act 5 Scene 1, lines 1–5)*

Shakespeare occasionally uses rhymed verse in *Much Ado About Nothing* to heighten theatrical effect and deepen the emotional and imaginative significance of a scene. For instance, he marks the sombre exit of Hero and her family (Act 4 Scene 1, lines 244–7) and the coming of dawn (Act 5 Scene 3, lines 24–7) with rhyming quatrains ABAB. Shakespeare will sometimes mark a character's exit from a scene with a concluding couplet, as he does for Hero in Act 3 Scene 1 (lines 105–6).

Songs

Balthasar's song, 'Sigh no more, ladies' (Act 2 Scene 3), comes at one of the turning points in the Beatrice–Benedick plot, sounding a mocking echo to one of the central preoccupations of the play: deception and 'The fraud of men'. The antithetical refrain ('blithe and bonny' – 'sounds of woe') also hints at the light and dark elements in the play. The song may originally have been sung badly, as both Don Pedro and Benedick's comments suggest. Or it may have been a movingly beautiful rendition, despite their criticisms, thereby adding one more dissonance between language and reality to the play.

Benedick's song, 'The God of love' (Act 5 Scene 2), is undoubtedly badly sung, as even Benedick has to admit. The words are supposedly spoken by a sad lover asking for pity from his hard-hearted mistress. The song was well-known in Shakespeare's time and much imitated, so that the comedy of Benedick as melancholy lover would have been immediately apparent.

The funeral song, 'Pardon, goddess of the night' (Act 5 Scene 3), provides an ironic fulfilment of Don Pedro's request for a serenade to Hero (Act 2 Scene 3, lines 77–8). Few critics have been impressed with the words: perhaps, as one critic suggested, Claudio and Don Pedro were just mediocre poets. In recent times, the song has been sung by groups of singers to great effect.

Traditional criticism

Criticism of *Much Ado About Nothing* in the two centuries following its first performance typically took the form of rather generalised praise for its entertaining comedy, discussion of plot and character, and comments about the moral insights to be found in the two love stories. Beatrice and Benedick's encounters were enjoyed from the start. For example, David Erskine Baker remarked in 1764:

> This comedy, tho' not free from faults, has nevertheless numberless beauties in it, nor is there perhaps in any play so pleasing a match of wit and repartee as is supported between Benedict [*sic*] and Beatrice in this, and the contrivance of making them fall in love with one another, who had both equally forsworn that passion, is very ingeniously conducted.

The leading eighteenth-century critic, Doctor Samuel Johnson, admired the apparent ease with which Shakespeare wrote comedy, in which 'he seems to repose, or to luxuriate, as in a mode of thinking congenial to his nature'. He also approved of Shakespeare's predilection for mingling comedy and tragedy in his plays, as for example in *Much Ado About Nothing*. Johnson believed writing for the theatre should have a moral purpose and felt that Shakespeare's 'mingled drama' combined the instructive qualities of both tragedy and comedy.

William Hazlitt, writing in 1817, was impressed by Hero's beauty, tenderness and 'the admired trial of her love'. He felt Claudio's confession of his admiration for Hero was 'as pleasing an image of the entrance of love into a youthful bosom as can well be imagined'. Perhaps influenced by the Romantics' belief in the essential goodness of human nature, he was (by later critics' standards) remarkably non-judgemental in his assessment of Claudio's behaviour. He seems unconcerned that Claudio 'divorces [Hero] in the very marriage ceremony' and shows no unease about the 'temporary consignment to the grave' which restores her 'to the confidence and the arms of her lover'.

In the late eighteenth and nineteenth centuries, most critics saw the comedies as light-hearted, romantic works and discussed the characters as if they were real people, passing moral judgements on their behaviour. Beatrice and Benedick were criticised for their aggressive speech, 'conceited' wit and rapid changes of mood. Beatrice was sometimes condemned as 'an odious woman', too masculine and aggressive, while critics (mostly male) saw in Hero their ideal woman: passive, demure and obedient. Debate, however, increasingly focused on the motives and actions of Hero and Claudio. Charles Swinburne pondered over 'the doubtfully desirable consummation' of Hero and Claudio's ultimate marriage, while Georg Brandes, writing in 1895, was even more harshly critical:

> If ever man was unworthy a woman's love, that man is
> Claudio. If ever marriage was odious and ill-omened, this is it.

Brandes was also one of the first to identify problems of structure, style, and overall effect in *Much Ado About Nothing*, matters which were increasingly to preoccupy twentieth-century critics. So, for example, he justified Shakespeare making Claudio such a contemptible young man because only then 'could the enchanting personality of Beatrice shine forth in its fullest splendour'.

In the first half of the twentieth century, studies such as H B Charlton's *Shakespearian Comedy* (1938) tended to see the comedies in terms of 'universal' (and frequently paired) themes: appearance and reality, wooing and wedding, romance and realism, innocence and experience, order and disorder. Most early twentieth-century critics continued to regard Shakespeare's comedies as 'happy' plays, offering escapist, romantic, sentimental entertainment. The plays also continued to be read as revelations of character, influenced in large part by the approach of A C Bradley in his *Shakespearian Tragedy* (1904), but also by new ideas from Freudian psychology.

The pioneering work of Caroline Spurgeon on the imagery in Shakespeare's plays ensured that most subsequent critics have in some way discussed the images in *Much Ado About Nothing*. She notes 'what a wealth of lively images there are in this play': light, sound, swift movement, dancing, music, song, riding, galloping, ambling, birds and greyhounds – all very fitting for Beatrice's high spirits. Spurgeon also feels that a sense of the aristocracy at play is created by all the sporting images: angling, archery, fencing, falconry, hunting, hare-coursing, gambling, bear-baiting.

From the 1950s onwards, a strand of criticism developed which interpreted Shakespearian comedy as the expression of a society's myths and rituals. Northrop Frye saw one recurring pattern in comedies such as *A Midsummer Night's Dream* and *As You Like It*: a double setting with a movement from the disordered and threatening city or court world into a 'green world', often represented by the forest or countryside, ending with the establishment of a renewed society, frequently represented by marriage. Sherman Hawkins saw an alternative recurring pattern in plays like *Much Ado About Nothing* and *Twelfth Night*. Here there is a single setting and the characters stay put, but they are visited by outsiders, who upset the routine of the community into which they come. Often the intruders belong to one sex, the inhabitants to another. Obstacles to love in this world are not external (like rival suitors, disapproving parents, etc.), but come from the lovers themselves. Thus Beatrice–Benedick and Hero–Claudio represent, each in their own way, the 'war' of the sexes. Like the 'green world' pattern comedies, Hawkins saw these single-setting comedies ending with the establishment of a renewed and harmonious society, symbolised by marriage.

Barbara Everett, however, sees little sense of 'holiday' or 'timeless pleasure' in Messina. For her, *Much Ado About Nothing* is a 'serious' comedy:

> The play concerns itself with what can only be called the most mundane or 'local' fact in that world of love that the comedies create: that is, that men and women have a notably different character, different mode of thinking, different system of loyalties, and, particularly, different social place and function. Not only this; but this is the first play in which the clash of these two worlds is treated with a degree of seriousness, and in which the woman's world dominates.

Everett sees the atmosphere in Leonato's house as 'one of ennobled domesticity', a world with 'a sense of habitual reality in a familiar social group', a world largely feminine in character. Into this world 'come the warriors, covered with masculine honours, cheerful with victory, and heralded importantly by a messenger'. This 'company of young bloods, headed by the noble Don Pedro . . . all hold together with a cheerful masculine solidarity'. Events in the play, however, move Benedick to desert his 'sworn brothers' and 'cross the boundaries of a world of masculine domination'. At the end of the play, while Hero 'lives', other things do seem to die: 'part of an old romantic ideal, and a sense of easy loyalty between young men'. Yet other things take the place of what is lost:

> a wisdom, balance, and generosity of mind and feeling, largely expressed through the women's roles

An example of criticism which uses a particular concept or theme to approach the play is that of Ralph Berry. Berry sees illusion as 'the grand theme' running through nearly all the comedies, together with its antithesis, reality. He identifies a spectrum of 'illusion-themes', explored to varying degrees in different plays. At one end of the spectrum are mistaken identity and deception, which he feels are the most insistent qualities of *Much Ado About Nothing*. At the other are follies of fantasy, self-deception and rational failure to recognise fraud and deceptive appearance (all of which can of course also be detected in the play). As such, Berry's spectrum seems to have been predicted in A P Rossiter's assertion about the play that

> misapprehensions, misprisions, misunderstandings, misinterpretations and misapplications are the best names for what the comedy as a whole is 'about'

Berry also argues that Shakespeare in his more mature comedies was experimenting with a new approach to the comic genre: 'the construction of two distinct plays within one frame'. At a time when 'nothing' and 'noting' were similarly pronounced, the very title of *Much Ado About Nothing* would sound ambiguous to his audience, suggesting both a 'jolly elaboration' (nothing), and a 'serious analysis of modes of knowing' (noting). The variety of interpretations of the play in performance (see pages 98–101) suggests that both features are indeed present and make for entertaining and thought-provoking theatre.

For Berry, *Much Ado About Nothing*'s major concern is with 'problems of knowing', and is signalled in the opening line (Leonato's

'I learn in this letter'). 'Love' may be the most commonly occurring lexical item (90 times), but clusters of the 'know' word occur almost as often (84 times) and at significant moments. No other Shakespearian comedy has more occurrences. Berry sees the play as having three interwoven plots (Hero–Claudio, Beatrice–Benedick and Dogberry–Borachio), each exploring and articulating different aspects of the problem of distinguishing truth from illusion. Every situation, every deliberate deception, every eavesdropping, tests a character's ability to judge and assess the evidence of their eyes and ears:

> [Shakespeare] poses always the question: how do I know? How can I be sure that A is telling the truth, that B is a villain, that C loves me, that D is lovesick? How can intuition be confirmed? These variants of the central question are exhibited, with complete mastery, in virtually every scene in *Much Ado About Nothing* . . .'Know' is the conceptual principle of the play.

Modern criticism

Since the 1970s, new critical approaches to Shakespeare have radically challenged the style and assumptions of the earlier criticism outlined above. The new critical approaches argue that traditional interpretations, with their focus on character, imagery and theme, are misleading. The assumption that underlies most criticism before the 1970s is that a play's meanings – or themes – are somehow 'in' the text and that these hidden meanings can be discovered through a close study of the text itself. Much post-1970s criticism, while acknowledging the importance of close reading, sees meaning in a text as being 'constructed' not 'found'. It is what the reader brings to the text and the particular social, political and economic pressures on the text when it was written that creates meaning. Such critics argue that the traditional concentration on personal feelings results in a spurious objectivity which ignores society and history, and so divorces literary, dramatic and aesthetic matters from their social context. This detachment from the real world makes traditional criticism elitist, sexist and unpolitical.

Modern critical perspectives therefore shift the focus from individuals to how social conditions (of both the world of the play and of Shakespeare's England) are reflected in characters' relationships, language and behaviour. Modern criticism also concerns itself with how changing social assumptions at different periods in post-Elizabethan history have affected interpretations of the play. Penny Gay, for example (see below, pages 95–6), looks at how *Much Ado About Nothing* and other comedies have been staged over the past 50 years when perceptions of gender have undergone massive changes.

Like traditional criticism, the new critical perspectives include many different approaches but share common features. Modern criticism:

- is sceptical of 'character' approaches (but often uses them);
- concentrates on political, social and economic factors, arguing that these factors determined Shakespeare's creativity and influence audiences' and critics' interpretations;
- identifies contradictions, fragmentation and disunity in the plays;
- questions the possibility of 'happy' or 'hopeful' endings to the comedies, preferring ambiguous, unsettling or sombre ones;
- produces readings that are subversive of existing social structures;
- identifies how the plays express the interests of dominant groups, particularly rich and powerful males;
- insists that 'theory' (psychological, social, economic, etc.) is essential to produce valid readings;
- often expresses its commitment to particular causes or perspectives (e.g. to feminism, or equality, or political change);
- argues that all readings are political or ideological readings and that traditional criticism falsely claims to be objective;
- argues that traditional approaches have always interpreted Shakespeare conservatively, in ways that confirm and maintain the interests of the elite or dominant class.

Interestingly, *Much Ado About Nothing* has received less attention from the new radical critics than, for example, *Twelfth Night*, but certain features of the play have proved attractive. The following discussion is organised under headings which represent major contemporary critical perspectives (political and feminist, performance, psychoanalytic, postmodern). But it is vital to appreciate that there is often overlap between the categories, and that to pigeonhole any example of criticism too precisely is to reduce its value and application.

Feminist and political criticism

It has become conventional to separate 'feminist' from 'political' criticism. But with *Much Ado About Nothing* it seems inappropriate to treat them as distinct categories. Apart from an occasional Marxist discussion (Elliot Krieger, for example, sees the play as Shakespeare's 'clearest dramatic treatment of the difficulty a ruling class faces in its attempt to isolate itself from inquiring into the traditions and appearances on which it has constructed its scale of values'), in practice both forms of criticism are understandably interlinked, most typically by the notion of patriarchy (male domination of women) and misogyny (hatred of women), as the following account demonstrates.

Political criticism is a convenient label for approaches concerned with power and social structure: in the world of the play, in Shakespeare's time and in our own. *Much Ado About Nothing* may be centrally concerned with love but, nonetheless, various interpretations, both in criticism and in stage productions, have highlighted 'political' aspects of the play, nearly always to do with gender. As Marilyn Williamson (see pages 96–7) asserts, 'The fact that the comedies are about love and personal themes does not preclude their also being about power.'

Feminism aims to achieve rights and equality for women in social, political and economic life. It challenges sexist beliefs and practices which result in the degradation, oppression and subordination of women. Feminist critics therefore reject 'male ownership' of criticism in which men determined what questions were to be asked of a play, and which answers were acceptable. They argue that male criticism often distorts women's points of view.

Shakespeare's comedies hold special interest for feminist critics. Unlike the tragedies or histories, female characters have the major parts and speak as many lines as the men. Like Beatrice, they are witty and intelligent, more than holding their own with men in dialogue, and their actions powerfully influence or direct the development of plot. Like Beatrice, they often appear to be independent spirits, free to act in their dramatic worlds, apparently unshackled by father, husband or lover.

Feminist criticism, like any 'approach', takes a wide variety of forms. For some, Shakespeare is seen as 'feminist in sympathy'. Juliet Dusinberre contrasts the infatuated idolatry of Hero and Claudio with the 'reasoned' love of Beatrice and Benedick, which is capable of surviving in the adult world far better than the 'idolatries of youth'. She concludes:

> Shakespeare saw men and women as equals in a world which declared them unequal. He did not divide human nature into the masculine and the feminine, but observed in the individual man or woman an infinite variety of union between opposing impulses. To talk about Shakespeare's women is to talk about his men, because he refused to separate their worlds physically, intellectually, or spiritually.

More sceptical feminist critics, however, point to what they see as the comedies' often hidden patriarchal assumptions, which in Shakespeare's day still overwhelmingly marginalised women. Carol Thomas Neely sees the world of *Much Ado About Nothing* as a patriarchal and militaristic society almost entirely driven and controlled by men. The bawdy wit, especially the cuckoldry jokes, affirms sexuality as the central component of marriage and emphasises male power and female weakness. Hero approaches her marriage with a heart that 'is exceeding heavy' and flinches at being 'heavier soon by the weight of a man'; Margaret asks Benedick to 'Give us our swords; we have bucklers of our own.' Neely sees Beatrice's betrothal kiss and subsequent silence as

> marking the beginning of the inequality that Beatrice feared in marriage and that is also implicit in the framing of the wedding festivities with male jokes about cuckoldry, in the re-establishment of male authority by means of these jokes, and in Benedick's control of the nuptials.

Penny Gay believes Shakespeare was particularly interested in the workings of gender in *Much Ado About Nothing* and chose to centre his comedies around 'transgressive female figures [like Beatrice] who, though politically powerless, can refuse to obey the rules of appropriate gender behaviour, flaunting her sexual mystery as if to point out that the patriarchy cannot do without her'. Like Everett (see pages 90–1), she believes that *Much Ado About Nothing* 'insists from its opening lines that the audience recognise it as taking place in the "real world", with its townsfolk, householders and their families, servants and visitors – and its gossip'. She sees Messina as a society structured very like the Elizabethan one which first witnessed it, 'in which the niceties of interpersonal behaviour are directed by accepted rules'.

For Gay, the Hero–Claudio story demonstrates the gap between idealism and reality, showing two lovers fully accepting the behavioural restrictions of conventional Elizabethan gender roles, with near-disastrous consequences. The Beatrice–Benedick story in contrast shows how two strong-willed characters can resist being confined by those same gender roles. They may, when they admit their sexual attraction, fall into society's romantic love behaviour (i.e. sonnets, sickness, etc.), but they meet their fate 'with wit, fully conscious of their own absurdity: "Thou and I are too wise to woo peaceably."'

She argues that the play triumphs by persuading the audience to believe in a conservative 'vision of a community always to be revitalised from within, by the incorporation of rebellious energy, not its expulsion'. It does this by flattering the audience's intelligence, suggesting that marriage is not just for dull people like the callow, foolish, conventional Claudio (and, to a lesser extent, Hero), but also for witty, unconventional people like Beatrice and Benedick.

In an age acutely aware of the workings of power and politics, the actions of Don Pedro and his bastard brother would have seemed familiar to many in Shakespeare's audience. Traditional criticism assumes that Don Pedro's deceptions are obviously benevolent, while Don John's are 'evil'. However, Jean Howard questions which is the greatest crime: Don John's plan to slander Hero's reputation, Don Pedro's to marry her off to a count when she expected a prince, or Leonato's to entrust his daughter to a man who had branded her a whore. Don John may initiate the plot which 'kills' Hero, but it is male misogyny that allows him to succeed. In the world of Messina, Howard concludes, manipulation and deception are acceptable when practised by legitimate male privilege, but 'evil' when practised by women and 'bastards' (outsiders). Don John and innate female moral frailty are therefore made the play's scapegoats for the failings of a misogynistic patriarchy.

Marilyn Williamson sees marriage as a significant power relationship within the plays: 'As the comedies drive towards marriage, the men look forward to social advancement and the women to subordination'. So, for example, marriage for both Claudio and Benedick means 'entry into full membership within society', but for Hero and Beatrice it means silence and obedience.

Williamson also believes that the numerous cuckolding jokes, which sound so strange to modern ears, provide an insight into the power relationships within *Much Ado About Nothing*. The capacity to make her husband a cuckold was the one power an Elizabethan wife had in relation to her husband. So while marriage might confer status on a man, it also carried a new threat to his identity – the shame of becoming a cuckold. As soon as Benedick hears Claudio talk of Hero as his future wife, he begins to use horn images. Williamson sees the male cuckolding jokes that run throughout the play as feeding and reinforcing the men's distrust of women and anxiety about their own loss of identity and honour. Such an attitude 'forms a context in which Claudio's suspicions of Hero are credible on very flimsy evidence'.

The one woman with power is, of course, Beatrice, 'whose tongue is her weapon'. From the start of the play she consistently intrudes on male territory. She mocks their military attitudes, makes her own cuckolding jokes, separates Benedick from his male friends. She demands that Benedick kill Claudio, pointing out the flimsy evidence against Hero, wishing herself to be a man. Once Benedick has made his choice at the church, he 'never returns to the old male camaraderie, with its pejorative view of marriage, after Hero's name is cleared'. In the final scene, when Claudio tries to restore him to good humour with yet more horn joking, Benedick emphatically puts him down (Act 5 Scene 4, lines 40–51).

One difference between modern critics like Williamson and earlier traditional critics can be seen in their contrasting interpretations of the endings of the comedies. Typically, traditional critics offer a conservative view, arguing that subversive energies may be liberated in the comedies but the ending brings these energies back into control. After a period of holiday or festival, social relationships return to how they were at the start. For Williamson, however, order may apparently be restored at the end of the play, but the questions raised by the comedy do not go away – indeed, the audience may well feel disturbed and uneasy in its response to the resolution. How could Hero accept Claudio the second time? Is Beatrice truly happy to marry Benedick? Williamson certainly sees 'the work of ideology' in the ending of *Much Ado About Nothing*: Beatrice and Benedick must marry because any other outcome would 'disturb the smooth surface of the newly reconciled society'.

Performance criticism

Performance criticism fully acknowledges that *Much Ado About Nothing* is a play: a script to be performed by actors to an audience. It examines all aspects of the play in performance: its staging in the theatre or on film and video. Performance criticism focuses on Shakespeare's stagecraft and the semiotics of theatre (signs: words, costumes, gestures, etc.), together with the 'afterlife' of the play (what happened to *Much Ado About Nothing* after Shakespeare wrote it). That involves scrutiny of how productions at different periods have presented the play. As such, performance criticism appraises how the text has been cut, added to, rewritten and rearranged to present a version felt appropriate to a given period.

The 1600 Quarto edition of *Much Ado About Nothing* states that the play 'had been sundry times publicly acted', but the only performance in Shakespeare's lifetime for which there is documentary evidence took place in 1613. Until the Puritans closed the theatres in 1642, it was undoubtedly a popular play, as Leonard Digges' verse introducing the 1640 edition of Shakespeare's poems testifies. That Digges specifically mentions Beatrice and Benedick suggests there was a strong interest in the transgression of gender norms in the early seventeenth century, particularly by strong, witty and insubordinate women who probably both worried and fascinated contemporary audiences. They would have enjoyed watching Benedick, the seemingly arch-misogynist and spokesman for traditional patriarchal values, meet his match in Beatrice, the articulate, assertive, independent woman. A reference by Robert Burton in 1624 to couples who 'are harsh and ready to disagree, offended with each other's carriage, like Benedict and Betteris (*sic*) in the Comedy' also suggests that the 'merry war' was played on the early seventeenth-century stage in a rather aggressive manner.

The Hero–Claudio story also clearly appealed to contemporary audiences. Seventeen variants of the legend have been traced to the period. Men perhaps appreciated the image of silent submissive womanhood, while women saw a picture of female suffering. The Watch scenes seem also to have been very popular, because at least nine plays in the early seventeenth century introduced a Constable and Watch.

As in Shakespeare's time, the staging conventions of seventeenth-century theatres were mainly non-naturalistic, with no scenery except for a few movable props (e.g. a bench for the Watch or an 'arbour' for the gulling scenes). As John Cox remarks, the value of such an acting space was that it

> ensured the primacy of the spoken word, important in a play with so much verbal elaboration [and] heightened awareness of the play as performance, an important effect in a comedy which foregrounds masking, theatricality, the acting of roles, and the uncertain boundaries between illusion and reality.

Cox identifies certain artifices of seventeenth-century staging, for example, speaking directly to the audience in soliloquy or aside, or the convention that actors may be inaudible or invisible to others on stage, or that masquerade disguises genuinely work. He argues that these conventions would have

> accorded well with the elements of artifice in the play: its elaborate verbal conceits, its contrivances of plot (e.g. the gulling of Benedick and Beatrice), and the conventionalisation of the Hero–Claudio story. In the social relations of Leonato's house there is nearly always an overlay of artifice, of disingenuousness; witty indirection is a mark of social sophistication.

Audiences of the late seventeenth-century Restoration period did not much like romantic comedy and *Much Ado About Nothing* fell out of favour. There are no records of the play being staged until well into the eighteenth century, when the rise of new bourgeois theatre audiences with a liking for romantic plays endorsing a moral message of mutual love and marriage helped it to come back into popular esteem. Between 1747 and 1776, David Garrick staged the play more often than any other Shakespearian comedy. His productions were swift, lively and entertaining, with Beatrice and Benedick the dominant interest. Average playing time was under two hours and substantial cuts were made in the script. Garrick and his leading ladies played the 'merry war' as an aggressively vigorous battle for supremacy.

The nineteenth century paid more attention to visual effect, with rich costumes and scenery. The opening scene of *Much Ado About Nothing* would typically show Leonato's palatial house and garden with views of the town and harbour of Messina. Productions used many elaborate scene changes and special staging effects, so that, despite heavy cuts to the script, performances could take as much as four hours. The end result was that the primacy of the actor and the spoken word was lost amidst the spectacle and 'authentic realism'.

The dominant mood of Victorian productions was of romantic happiness, with only slight emphasis on the darker elements of the play. Most leading actors of the period showed a strong interest in motivation and character development, indicating, for example, an unconscious attraction between Beatrice and Benedick from the beginning of the play. Henry Irving played Benedick as a slightly eccentric older man, reacting to Beatrice in the early scenes with 'good-natured, half-amused tolerance'. Many Victorians were uneasy about Beatrice's 'masculine energy' and the most admired Beatrices of the period were those who softened her aggressiveness to resemble more the nineteenth-century stereotype of ideal womanhood: sweet, gentle and delicate. Most commonly, Beatrice's aggressive wit was explained away as being a mask which hid 'the tender heart beneath'.

The early twentieth century saw a return to much simpler stagings of the play. Most productions no longer attempted to create an impression of realism. Under the influence of William Poel and Harley Granville Barker, the stage was cleared of the clutter of historical detail. The aim was to recapture the conditions of the Elizabethan bare stage, which was not concerned with theatrical illusion. That implied simple impressionistic sets, continuous action, lightly cut scripts and a concern for clear speaking of Shakespeare's language.

The feminist revolution, from the 1960s onwards, had a profound influence on productions of the play, radically changing the representation of Beatrice and foregrounding both gender issues and patriarchal attitudes. Penny Gay's study (see pages 95–6) includes a perceptive account of how the heroines at the centre of Shakespeare's comedies have been embodied in stage performances in Britain since the Second World War. Whereas Beatrices in the 1950s had conformed more to nineteenth-century stereotypes of the warm, gentle, feminine woman, later Beatrices became increasingly 'unruly', contesting in various ways conventional female stereoypes. Some Beatrices were sharply aggressive, others challenged patriarchal values more subtly. Most established superiority over their Benedicks.

Late twentieth-century productions often placed strong emphasis on the dark elements in *Much Ado About Nothing*: the mistreatment of Hero, the malice of Don John, Claudio's behaviour, the male attitudes at the disrupted wedding, the gender inequalities of Messina society. Some productions emphasised the masks, deceptions and playing of roles. One Benedick arrived from the wars with his head covered in a blood-stained bandage, which he removed when everyone had gone to reveal no trace of a wound.

Di Trevis' 1988 production offered a scathing criticism of modern affluence from a feminist perspective. It was set in a world of wealth and privilege and opened with characters sun-bathing on the terrace of Leonato's multi-million pound mansion. Beatrice was a physically formidable Amazonian woman who 'strode the stage in complete control' (*Observer*). In the masked dance she swung a diminutive balding Benedick across her back and threw him about. The mistreatment of Hero was heavily emphasised and Claudio played in a more than usually unlikeable fashion, while Don John, the outsider, was treated not unsympathetically. At the disrupted wedding, Leonato turned savagely on his speechless daughter. One critic wrote: 'Here is the patriarchy, as a conspiracy of husbands and fathers, in full, unquestioning cry'. The traditional happy ending was chillingly questioned – everyone was dressed in black.

A study of the performance history of *Much Ado About Nothing* shows that each age has tried to 'mould' the play to suit its own cultural norms. This is especially apparent in the persistent ambiguity with which Beatrice has been viewed. As noted earlier, eighteenth-century audiences enjoyed Beatrice for her aggressive wit, and her story was presented as a moral lesson on the value of love and marriage; most nineteenth-century productions softened Beatrice's aggression and heightened her capacity for 'feeling'; the gender revolution of the late twentieth century brought about a reversal in her presentation, with actresses now highlighting her independence and assertiveness.

Yet, while each age has seen elements in the play to accord with its own beliefs, the play remains firmly a product of late Elizabethan culture. Just as the nineteenth century could not conceive of a 'masculine' Beatrice, so the late twentieth century often found it hard to imagine Beatrice 'taming [her] wild heart to [Benedick's] loving hand' and speculated over the reasons for her final silence.

Psychoanalytic criticism

In the twentieth century, psychoanalysis became a major influence on the understanding and interpretation of human behaviour. The founder of psychoanalysis, Sigmund Freud, explained personality as the result of unconscious and irrational desires, repressing memories or wishes, sexuality, fantasy, anxiety and conflict. Freud's theories have had a strong influence on the criticism and staging of Shakespeare's plays, most obviously on *Hamlet* in the well-known claim that Hamlet suffers from an Oedipus complex.

Some psychoanalytic criticism of *Much Ado About Nothing* has commented on the interaction of violence and love, idealisation and degradation, in Claudio's attraction to Hero and his subsequent rejection of her. Joseph Westlund argues that Claudio idealises Hero and, in doing so, denies her sexuality, loving her 'as a brother to his sister' (Act 4 Scene 1, line 47). When her sexuality emerges, he feels deceived and insecure, and so violently rejects her. Harry Berger sees a certain sibling rivalry in Hero's attitude to her cousin and believes her criticisms of Beatrice in the gulling scene (Act 3 Scene 1) are not pretended, but a sign of genuine envy and disapproval. Carol Thomas Neely sees Messina as a deeply repressive world of patriarchy and militarism, where fear of commitment and the consequent loss of power is expressed through either misogyny, idealisation of love, sexual anxiety or social conventionality.

An obvious character for psychoanalytic interpretation is Don John, whose motiveless malevolence suggests a psychopathic personality, and such an intepretation has sometimes been seen in stage productions. As John Cox notes, instead of the traditional and unproblematic solitary malcontent or scheming villain, Don John has 'been played with greater depth as a jealous or melancholic psychopath, sometimes with a physical disability or a compulsive twitch or stammer'.

Postmodern criticism

Postmodern criticism (sometimes called 'deconstruction' or 'poststructuralism') is not always easy to understand because it is not centrally concerned with consistency or reasoned argument. It does not accept that one section of the story is necessarily connected to what follows, or that characters relate to each other in meaningful ways. Because of such assumptions, postmodern criticism is sometimes described as 'reading against the grain'. The approach therefore has obvious drawbacks in providing a model for examination students who are expected to display reasoned coherent argument and respect for the evidence of the text.

Postmodern approaches to *Much Ado About Nothing* are most clearly seen in stage productions. There you could think of it as simply a 'mixture of styles', with little regard shown for consistency in character or for coherence in telling the story, and characters are dressed in costumes from very different historical periods. Ironically, Shakespeare himself has been regarded as a postmodern writer in the way he mixes genres in his plays, comedy with tragedy.

Much Ado About Nothing has not proved attractive to postmodern critics. Terry Eagleton, for example, in his influential *William Shakespeare* (1986) makes only two brief passing references. The first that 'language, once touched by . . . desire, tends to run riot' (as Benedick remarks about Claudio in love, 'his words are a very fantastical banquet'). The second is to the effect that it is impossible to decide whether the 'elaborately fictitious information' fed to Benedick and Beatrice 'uncovers' their love or 'actually constructs it'.

Conclusion

Barbara Everett, whose earlier work has already been discussed on pages 90–1, shows in a more recent study (2001) how it is possible to balance both traditional and modern approaches. She focuses particularly on character and the psychological complexities of the play, how it is paradoxically both about 'nothing' and 'everything'. For Everett, Beatrice is 'Shakespeare's true heroine, the sharp and comical child of sorrow'. Like Doctor Johnson in the eighteenth century, she too admires how the play mimics real life in showing the co-existence of happiness and unhappiness:

> [Shakespeare's] art recognises the interdependence of the dark
> and the light in life, especially at those points of love and
> friendship where feeling is most acute, and often most
> complex. The mature comedies seek to perfect a style or
> condition in which happiness exists not just despite
> unhappiness but through it, because of it, yet charitably and
> sympathetically, like Patience smiling at grief. There must in
> the end be the co-existence, the smiling and the grief.

Organising your responses

The purpose of this section is to help you improve your writing about *Much Ado About Nothing*. It offers practical guidance on two kinds of tasks: writing about an extract from the play and writing an essay. Whether you are answering an examination question, preparing coursework (term papers), or carrying out research into your own chosen topic, this section will help you organise and present your responses.

In all your writing, there are three vital things to remember:

- *Much Ado About Nothing* is a play. Although it is usually referred to as a 'text', *Much Ado About Nothing* is not a book, but a script intended to be acted on a stage. So your writing should demonstrate an awareness of the play in performance as theatre. That means you should always try to read the play with an 'inner eye', thinking about how it could look and sound on stage.

- *Much Ado About Nothing* is not a presentation of 'reality'. It is a dramatic construct in which the playwright, through theatre, engages the emotions and intellect of the audience. A major part of your task is to show how Shakespeare achieves his dramatic effects that so engage the audience. Through discussion of his handling of language, character and plot, your writing reveals how Shakespeare uses themes and ideas, attitudes and values, to give insight into crucial social, moral and political dilemmas of his time – and yours.

- How Shakespeare learned his craft. As a schoolboy, and in his early years as a dramatist, Shakespeare used all kinds of models or frameworks to guide his writing. But he quickly learned how to vary and adapt the models to his own dramatic purposes. This section offers frameworks that you can use to structure your writing. As you use them, follow Shakespeare's example! Adapt them to suit your own writing style and needs.

Writing about an extract

It is an expected part of all Shakespeare study that you should be able to write well about an extract (sometimes called a 'passage') from the play. An extract is usually between 30 and 70 lines long, and you are invited to comment on it. The instructions vary. Sometimes the task

is very briefly expressed:
- Write a detailed commentary on the following passage.
- Write about the effect of the extract on your own thoughts and feelings.

At other times a particular focus is specified for your writing:
- With close reference to the language and imagery of the passage, show in what ways it helps to establish important issues in the play.
- Analyse the style and structure of the extract, showing what it contributes to your appreciation of the play's major concerns.

In writing your response, you must of course take account of the precise wording of the task, and ensure you concentrate on each particular point specified. But however the invitation to write about an extract is expressed, it requires you to comment in detail on the language. You should identify and evaluate how the language creates character, contributes to plot development, offers opportunities for dramatic effect and embodies crucial concerns of the play as a whole. These 'crucial concerns' are also referred to as the 'themes', or 'issues', or 'preoccupations' of the play.

The following framework is a guide to how you can write a detailed commentary on an extract. Writing a paragraph or more on each item will help you bring out the meaning and significance of the extract, and show how Shakespeare achieves his effects.

Paragraph 1: Locate the extract in the play and say who is on stage.
Paragraph 2: State what the extract is about and identify its structure.
Paragraph 3: Identify the mood or atmosphere of the extract.
Paragraphs 4–8:
    Diction (vocabulary)
    Imagery
    Antithesis
    Repetition
    Lists
These paragraphs analyse how Shakespeare achieves his effects. They concentrate on the language of the extract, showing the dramatic effect of each item, and how the language expresses crucial concerns of the play.
Paragraph 9: Staging opportunities
Paragraph 10: Conclusion

The following example uses the framework to show how the paragraphs making up the essay might be written. The framework headings (in bold), would not of course appear in your essay. They are presented only to help you see how the framework is used.

Extract

BENEDICK This can be no trick, the conference was sadly borne, they
    have the truth of this from Hero, they seem to pity the lady: it
    seems her affections have their full bent: love me? Why, it must
    be requited: I hear how I am censured, they say I will bear myself
    proudly, if I perceive the love come from her: they say too, that   5
    she will rather die than give any sign of affection: I did never
    think to marry, I must not seem proud, happy are they that hear
    their detractions, and can put them to mending: they say the lady
    is fair, 'tis a truth, I can bear them witness: and virtuous, 'tis so, I
    cannot reprove it: and wise, but for loving me: by my troth it is   10
    no addition to her wit, nor no great argument of her folly, for I
    will be horribly in love with her: I may chance have some odd
    quirks and remnants of wit broken on me, because I have railed
    so long against marriage: but doth not the appetite alter? A man
    loves the meat in his youth, that he cannot endure in his age.   15
    Shall quips and sentences, and these paper bullets of the brain
    awe a man from the career of his humour? No, the world must
    be peopled. When I said I would die a bachelor, I did not think I
    should live till I were married – here comes Beatrice: by this day,
    she's a fair lady, I do spy some marks of love in her.   20

Enter BEATRICE

BEATRICE Against my will I am sent to bid you come in to dinner.
BENEDICK Fair Beatrice, I thank you for your pains.
BEATRICE I took no more pains for those thanks, than you took pains
    to thank me, if it had been painful I would not have come.
BENEDICK You take pleasure then in the message.   25
BEATRICE Yea, just so much as you may take upon a knife's point, and
    choke a daw withal: you have no stomach, signor, fare you well.
                                                                   Exit
BENEDICK Ha, against my will I am sent to bid you come in to dinner:
    there's a double meaning in that: I took no more pains for those
    thanks than you take pains to thank me: that's as much as to say,   30
    any pains that I take for you is as easy as thanks: if I do not take

pity of her I am a villain, if I do not love her I am a Jew, I will go
get her picture. *Exit*

(Act 2 Scene 3, lines 181–213)

Paragraph 1: Locate the extract in the play and identify who is on stage.
Earlier in the play, Benedick had mused on the dramatic change love
had made to his friend Claudio and wondered whether he too might
be similarly transformed. He had concluded that no woman in the
world was perfect enough to tempt him into marriage. But his friends
set in motion the prince's plan to trick him into believing that Beatrice
harboured a secret passion for him. They allowed him to eavesdrop on
their conversation as they talked of her unhappy and unspoken love,
then left him alone to mull over what he had heard. This is the point
at which the extract begins, with Benedick alone on stage. Beatrice's
entrance is a result of Don Pedro's ruse to create further amusement
by sending her out to call Benedick into dinner.

Paragraph 2: State what the extract is about and identify its structure.
(Begin with one or two sentences identifying what the extract is about,
followed by several sentences briefly identifying its structure, that is,
the unfolding events and the different sections of the extract.)

The extract has three episodes: Benedick's soliloquy, Beatrice's
grudging invitation and Benedick's hopelessly optimistic
interpretation of her words. Shakespeare gives Benedick this soliloquy
to contrast with the one he speaks at the start of the scene. It reveals
his reaction to what he has just overheard. He is amazed by the news
but convinced it is true. Unhesitatingly he decides that Beatrice's love
for him must be returned in full and resolves to change his ways.
Beatrice now seems to him to possess all the virtues he would want in
a wife and he determines to 'be horribly in love with her'. He uneasily
anticipates being the butt of numerous jokes after having so long
spoken out against marrying, but emphatically defends his dramatic
and sudden change of mind.

Beatrice enters to call him into dinner. She is still smarting from
their last encounter when he had called her a Harpy, and she delivers
the invitation very grudgingly. Benedick, however, is convinced he
sees a loving meaning in her words.

Paragraph 3: Identify the mood or atmosphere of the extract.
Benedick's whole world has been turned upside down, just as the audience guessed and hoped would happen from the moment he boasted to his friends that they would never see him 'look pale with love'. His opening soliloquy is rich in comic irony as he desperately tries to rationalise his lightning transformation from self-satisfied scorner of love to shocked, confused lover. It is a delightful theatrical episode to watch the dubious logical arguments he employs to justify his own self-deception.

Shakespeare then deepens the comic irony by confronting the new Benedick with the old Beatrice: he looks to 'spy' signs of love in her, while she is impatiently dismissive of his unusually odd behaviour.

The end of the extract further intensifies the humour as the deluded lover attempts to see a hidden compliment ('double meaning') in Beatrice's scornful remarks.

Paragraph 4: Diction (vocabulary)
At the start of the extract, Benedick's customary playful use of words has deserted him – he is now serious, concerned and almost stunned. All he can manage for his opening statement is a series of simple monosyllables: 'This can be no trick'. When he recovers his composure a little, some of his linguistic spark returns with his use of the unexpected and emphatic 'horribly' and his talk of 'quips', 'sentences' (wise sayings), 'odd quirks' (jokes) and 'paper bullets of the brain' (harmless gibes). But the sight of Beatrice, his new-found love, proves too much for him. He now sounds just like the doting lover he once so despised: 'I thank you for your pains', 'I will go get her picture'.

Beatrice in contrast remains in full control of her words, taking up Benedick's use of 'pains' (i.e. care or concern) giving it a second meaning (hurt) and throwing it back again with interest: 'if it had been painful I would not have come'.

Paragraph 5: Imagery
Benedick's dramatic deflation is reflected in the imagery he uses. The only image in the first ten lines is an archery image: 'it seems her affections have their full bent' (i.e. stretched to their limit like a bow). Then, as he regains composure, something of the old Benedick returns. He argues that a man's opinions, like his taste in food, will

change as he grows older ('a man loves the meat in his youth . . .') and any jokes made against him will prove as harmless as 'paper bullets' because he is now firmly set on his new course ('career'), like a knight in armour charging in the lists. His final statement that he would be 'a Jew' (i.e. lacking in Christian love) if he did not love her, reflects the casual racism of the day towards Jews who were often subjected to abuse and religious persecution.

Beatrice remains on top form. When Benedick humbly asks her if she takes any pleasure in calling him to dinner, she says the pleasure is about as tiny as the piece of meat needed to 'choke a daw withal' ('daw' could mean a jackdaw or a simpleton). Her final sentence contains the insulting image she has directed at Benedick before: 'you have no stomach, signor' ('stomach' could mean either appetite or courage). She may be referring to Benedick's new meekness, feeling either triumphant or disappointed at the change in him.

Paragraph 6: Antithesis
The confident antitheses Benedick used in his earlier soliloquy to demonstrate his immunity to the charms of women are absent from the opening lines of this second soliloquy, but begin to return as he gathers his thoughts and attempts to find plausible reasons for his lightning change of heart: 'A man <u>loves</u> the meat in his <u>youth</u>, that he <u>cannot endure</u> in his <u>age</u>'; 'When I said I would <u>die</u> a <u>bachelor</u>, I did not think I should <u>live</u> till I were <u>married</u>'. But now his antitheses are being used to argue exactly the opposite to what he was saying only minutes before!

Paragraph 7: Repetition
The simple repeated subject–verb structure of the opening sentence (This can . . . the conference was . . . they have . . . they seem . . .) indicates Benedick's stunned reaction, while his repeated 'they say . . . they say . . .' shows how much he has taken his friends' criticisms to heart. The repetitions of 'pains' and 'thanks', used virtually as antitheses, as Benedick broods over Beatrice's words and the repeated pattern of his final sentence ('if I do not take pity of her I am a villain, if I do not love her I am a Jew, I will go get her picture') all suggest the mind of a man obsessed (and, in 'Jew', the casual racism of the times).

Paragraph 8: Lists
Benedick lists the qualities his friends have just attributed to Beatrice (fair, virtuous, wise), each time with a brief comment of his own and finishing with a half-joking criticism of himself (the following layout of the lines reveals how the list is structured):

they say the lady is fair,	'tis a truth, I can bear them witness:
and virtuous,	'tis so, I cannot reprove it:
and wise,	but for loving me

Benedick reveals an interestingly selective memory here. He recalls his friends saying Beatrice was 'fair' when in fact the prince said she was 'an excellent sweet lady'. Perhaps he heard what he wanted to hear, for he concedes in the very first scene of the play that she is a beautiful woman. Benedick also echoes his own earlier description of the ideal woman (rich, wise, virtuous, fair, mild, noble, of good discourse, an excellent musician), but now his list conveniently omits those qualities (rich, mild, noble) which do not apply to Beatrice.

Paragraph 9: Staging opportunities
The opening soliloquy is a challenging sequence for the actor playing the new 'horribly in love' Benedick. He must appear absurd yet be sincere, for he truly believes he loves Beatrice and this has turned his whole world upside down. He needs therefore to tread a fine line between seeming ridiculous and being sympathetic. The opening statement 'This can be no trick' can be delivered in a variety of ways: decisive, solemn, hesitant, puzzled, excited. From that point the actor must keep the drive of the soliloquy going through a range of emotions: sympathy for Beatrice's suffering, concern for her happiness, determination to behave better, wholehearted acceptance that he must 'be horribly in love with her'. Then come misgivings as he anticipates the ridicule he will get from his friends, until he finally convinces himself that loving Beatrice is exactly the right thing to do with the triumphant conclusion, 'The world must be peopled', a line which can often cause the audience to explode with laughter.

The soliloquy is drama at its most elemental: an actor and his audience. Many actors playing Benedick have directed their reactions to the audience in this extract, speaking the soliloquy as if arguing with a close friend, trying to justify their new opinions. Some members of Shakespeare's audience might have derived additional pleasure from recognising it as a parody of the rhetorical (persuasive) techniques they had learned at school. Modern productions often contrast Benedick's more extrovert reaction to what he has overheard with Beatrice's more intense and emotional response in the next scene.

The comedy of the dialogue with Beatrice depends very much on the incongruity of Benedick's spying 'marks of love' in her when there are plainly none to see. The greater her show of contempt, anger and sarcasm, the more comic are his attempts to be the loving suitor. Likewise, the more ferocious Beatrice's opening words are, the greater the audience's amusement as Benedick later attempts to see 'a double meaning' in them.

Paragraph 10: Conclusion
This extract sees the completion of the first part of Don Pedro's plan to 'bring Signor Benedick and the Lady Beatrice into a mountain of affection, th'one with th'other'. Benedick's soliloquy very much parallels and contrasts with Beatrice's reaction to her eavesdropping in the next scene.

It is comic to watch Benedick's friends deceive him into believing Beatrice is in love with him, but really he believes what he hears because he wants to believe it. His excuses are too feeble: ('the white-bearded fellow speaks it', 'they have the truth of this from Hero'). But in a sense he is right. Beatrice *does* love him: his heart has led him to be deceived into seeing the truth.

Reminders
- The framework is only a guide. It helps you to structure your writing. Use the framework for practice on other extracts. Adapt as you feel appropriate. Make it your own.
- Structure your response in paragraphs. Each paragraph makes a particular point and helps build up your argument.
- Focus tightly on the language, especially vocabulary, imagery, antithesis, lists, repetitions.

- Remember that *Much Ado About Nothing* is a play, a drama intended for performance. The purpose of writing about an extract is to identify how Shakespeare creates dramatic effect. What techniques does he use?
- Try to imagine the action. Visualise the scene in your mind's eye. But remember there can be many valid ways of performing a scene. Offer alternatives. Justify your own preferences by reference to the language.
- Who is on stage? Imagine their interaction. How do 'silent characters' react to what is said?
- Look for the theatrical qualities of the extract. What guides for actors' movement and expressions are given in the language? Comment on any stage directions.
- How might the audience respond? In Elizabethan times? Today? How might you respond as a member of the audience?
- How might the lines be spoken? Tone, emphasis, pace, pauses? Identify shifting moods and registers. Is the verse pattern smooth or broken, flowing or full of hesitations and abrupt turns?
- What is the importance of the extract in the play as a whole? Justify its thematic significance.
- Are there any 'key words'?
- How does the extract develop the plot, reveal character, deepen themes?
- In what ways can the extract be spoken/staged to reflect a particular interpretation?

Writing an essay

As part of your study of *Much Ado About Nothing* you will be asked to write essays, either under examination conditions or for coursework (term papers). Examinations mean that you are under pressure of time, usually having around one hour to prepare and write each essay. Coursework means that you have much longer to think about and produce your essay. But whatever the type of essay, each will require you to develop an argument about a particular aspect of *Much Ado About Nothing*.

The essays you write on *Much Ado About Nothing* require that you set out your thoughts on a particular aspect of the play, using evidence from the text. The people who read your essays (examiners, teachers, lecturers) will have certain expectations for your writing. In each essay they will expect you to discuss and analyse a particular topic, using evidence from the play to develop an argument in an organised, coherent and persuasive way. Examiners look for, and reward, what they call 'an informed personal response'. This simply means that you show you have good knowledge of the play ('informed') and can use evidence from it to support and justify your own viewpoint ('personal').

You can write about *Much Ado About Nothing* from different points of view. As pages 92–103 show, you can approach the play from a number of critical perspectives (feminist, political, psychoanalytic, etc.). You can also set the play in its historical context (social, literary, political, etc.) as shown in the Contexts section. You should write at different levels, moving beyond description to analysis and evaluation. Simply telling the story or describing characters is not as effective as analysing how events or characters embody wider concerns of the play. In *Much Ado About Nothing*, these 'wider concerns' (also called themes, issues, preoccupations – or more simply 'what the play is about') include: love (especially 'romantic' and 'realistic' love), deception, appearance and reality, women in a patriarchal world, male honour and female virtue, the interdependence of happiness and sorrow. In your writing, always give practical examples (quotations, actions) which illustrate the themes you discuss.

How should you answer an examination question or write a coursework essay? The following threefold structure can help you organise your response:

opening paragraph
developing paragraphs
concluding paragraph.

Opening paragraph. Begin with a paragraph identifying just what topic or issue you will focus on. Show that you have understood what the question is about. You probably will have prepared for particular topics. But look closely at the question and identify key words to see what particular aspect it asks you to write about. Adapt your material to answer that question. Examiners do not reward an essay, however well written, if it is not on the question set.

Developing paragraphs. This is the main body of your essay. In it, you develop your argument, point by point, paragraph by paragraph. Use evidence from the play that illuminates the topic or issue, and answers the question set. Each paragraph makes a point of dramatic or thematic significance. Some paragraphs could make points concerned with context or particular critical approaches. The effect of your argument builds up as each paragraph adds to the persuasive quality of your essay. Use brief quotations that support your argument, and show clearly just why they are relevant. Ensure that your essay demonstrates that you are aware that *Much Ado About Nothing* is a play, a drama intended for performance, and therefore open to a wide variety of interpretations and audience response.

Concluding paragraph. Your final paragraph pulls together your main conclusions. It does not simply repeat what you have written earlier, but summarises concisely how your essay has successfully answered the question.

The following notes show the 'ingredients' of an answer. In an examination it is usually helpful to prepare similar notes from which you write your essay, paragraph by paragraph. Remember that examiners are not impressed by 'name-dropping': use of critics' names. What they want you to show is your knowledge and judgement of the play and its contexts, and of how it has been interpreted from different critical perspectives.

Example

Question: How far do you agree with the statement that 'nothing is as it seems in *Much Ado About Nothing*?'

Opening paragraph
Show that you are aware how much the play is built around the idea that true knowledge is uncertain and that an individual's perception of

what he believes to be real is inevitably subjective. So include the following points and aim to write a sentence or more on each:

- The play's punning title on 'nothing' and 'noting' alerts the audience that there will be a lot of trouble with seeing, knowing and judging from appearances. Images of 'seeming/being' and clusters of the 'know' word occur almost as often as the 'love' word and at significant moments.
- Almost every character at some point in the play consciously assumes a role, pretending to be what he or she is not.
- Characters will deliberately attempt to deceive others, either benevolently (Don Pedro) or maliciously (Don John). The song 'Men were deceivers ever' and the cuckold jokes (where women are deceivers) also draw attention to the idea that deception is part of human nature.
- The fallibility of human nature also leads to errors of judgement. Characters leap to conclusions, misinterpreting what they see, their 'mistakings' caused by self-deception, self-delusion or limited intellect.
- The result is that (at one point or other in the play) nearly every character has to draw important inferences from what he or she sees, has been told or overhears. Nothing being 'what it seems' is a particularly acute problem in matters of love.

Developing paragraphs

Now write a paragraph on each of a number of different ways in which the play presents the problem of distinguishing truth from 'seeming truth'. In each paragraph identify the importance (dramatic, thematic, etc.) of the example you discuss. Some of the points you might include are given briefly below. At least one aspect of 'importance' is given in brackets, but there are of course others.

- Characters constantly assume roles to hide or deny their real identity or purpose (light-heartedly at the masked dance and in the gulling scenes where the prince, Hero and others play-act the part of concerned and candid friends; more seriously when Leonato plays the role of wronged father of a dead daughter and Hero pretends to be her father's niece).
- Characters assume roles to create a specific public image. (Don John claims to be unable to hide what he is, yet plays very successfully the concerned brother; Claudio changes almost

overnight from soldier to lover, then injured lover and finally repentant lover; Beatrice and Benedick are first scorners of love, then become courtly lovers and finally pretend to be reluctant bride and bridegroom.)

- Deliberate deception lies at the heart of the Hero–Claudio story. (Don Pedro's benevolent plot to woo Hero is countered by his brother's malicious scheming against Claudio at the masked dance and his more sinister plot to slander Hero's honour. Then follows Claudio and Don Pedro's scheme to sabotage the wedding, the Friar's plan to have Hero 'die', the false mourning rites and the masked betrothal.)

- Deliberate deception is also at the heart of the Beatrice–Benedick plot (started with the best of intentions by Don Pedro, who arranges for both Beatrice and Benedick to be deceived into eavesdropping on staged conversations).

- Characters are particularly vulnerable to self-deception or self-delusion in matters of love. (Benedick sees signs of love in Beatrice because he wants to, while Claudio believes what he sees at Hero's window because he fears to.)

- Misunderstandings arise through sheer dim-wittedness. (The Watch fail to realise the significance of the crime they have discovered; Dogberry remains to the very end looking for a non-existent thief with a padlock hanging from his ear.)

- Characters from the very start struggle to judge the truth of what they see or hear. (The Messenger and Leonato are momentarily puzzled by Beatrice's enquiry after Signor Mountanto; Claudio is unsure whether both Benedick and Don Pedro are not joking with him about Hero – 'You speak this to fetch me in, my lord'; Leonato has to judge carefully the accuracy of what Antonio's servant overhears.)

- The problem of knowing is also echoed in the language. (Claudio hesitantly asks Benedick if he 'noted' the daughter of Signor Leonato; Don Pedro diplomatically judges Leonato's invitation to stay at least a month to be sincerely meant – 'I dare swear he is no hypocrite, but prays from his heart'; at the wedding, Claudio savagely rails against Hero's 'exterior shows' of virtue which hide her inner corruption.)

- As events in the play become potentially tragic, the problem of knowing what is the truth becomes more crucial. (The Friar believes he has seen proof of Hero's innocence by careful 'noting of the lady', Claudio and Don Pedro in contrast rush to condemn her; Leonato immediately and unquestioningly accepts their judgement of his daughter as being 'a common stale'; Beatrice seeks to be certain of Benedick's love before daring to ask him to kill his friend.)

- The problem of knowing the truth of love is especially important for Beatrice and Benedick. (Hesitant and suspicious, by nature or through experience, they each need to be sure of the other's sincerity before making a commitment. They remain guarded and defensive to the last, protesting their lack of love even as they are betrothed.)

- The world of Messina is in some ways a flawed society: outwardly merry and tolerant, but concealing ugly stains of patriarchy and inequality (its mistreatment of women, its moral double standards, its concern with social hierarchy, its shallow, idle, ostentatious and selfish lifestyle).

Concluding paragraph

Write several sentences pulling together your conclusions. You might include the following points:

- The play raises the question that we all must face: how can we know the truth for certain? It gives at least three different answers:
  - The play's preoccupation with theatricality, trickery and outward show suggests that much of 'real' life is just an illusion (*Much Ado About Nothing*).
  - The play's theatricality and trickery suggests that knowing the truth for certain is a slippery and difficult business which requires careful 'noting' and that failing to do so can have potentially tragic consequences (*Much Ado About Noting*).
  - The final unmasking scene and dance suggests that truth will in the end be revealed through a combination of love, trust and loyalty. Beatrice believes in her 'soul' that Hero is innocent; Benedick trusts her judgement enough to risk his life. If only Claudio had trusted Hero when she whispered in his ear that he was 'in her heart'.

- Productions of the play in the last 50 years suggest that there is no one 'right' meaning. *Much Ado About Nothing* has been played convincingly in a range of interpretations, from delightfully sparkling comedy to dark moral satire, but all enjoy and exploit the play's ambiguity.

Writing about character

As the Critical approaches section showed, much critical writing about *Much Ado About Nothing* traditionally focused on characters, writing about them as if they were living human beings. Today it is not sufficient just to describe their personalities. When you write about characters you will also be expected to show that they are dramatic constructs, part of Shakespeare's stagecraft. They embody the wider concerns of the play, have certain dramatic functions, and are set in a social and political world with particular values and beliefs. They reflect and express issues of significance to Shakespeare's society – and today's.

All that may seem difficult and abstract. But don't feel overwhelmed. Everything you read in this Guide is written with those principles in mind, and can be a model for your own writing. Of course you should say what a character seems like to you, but you should also write about how Shakespeare makes them part of his overall dramatic design. For example, the play's essential ambiguity is reflected in the way Shakespeare repeatedly arranges his characters in doubles to create comparisons and contrasts:

- Benedick and Claudio are two male friends and comrades in war, the first more cynical and the second less experienced. Beatrice and Hero are virtual sisters, linked in love and devotion but very different in personality. Dogberry has his loyal friend and sidekick Verges, their attempts at impressive language a comic parody of their more articulate superiors.

- Leonato and Antonio are elderly brothers united in loyalty, while Don Pedro and Don John are brothers divided by enmity. The prince and his half-brother are both inveterate plotters. Don Pedro tries to set up marriages, while Don John tries to destroy them. Both brothers have their band of 'henchmen' to assist them in their plotting.

- The two comrades in war each fall in love with one of the 'sisters', their pairings ominously echoed by Margaret and Borachio, light-heartedly by the masked dancers.

Shakespeare also heightens the confusions in the play by weaving his characters into the two main plots in the most complex of ways. For example, Benedick is deceived by Don Pedro and Claudio, who are both in turn deceived by Don John into denouncing Hero, which provokes Beatrice, already deceived by her cousin Hero, to demand that her new lover Benedick challenge his old friend Claudio.

In a play with complex plots, a number of characters will inevitably do little more than fulfil a plot function. Antonio provides an imaginary niece, Margaret impersonates Hero, the Friar suggests the plan for Hero's 'rebirth', Borachio devises the plan to slander Hero, Conrade provokes Borachio's boasting, the Watch overhear and apprehend, Ursula helps to trick Beatrice, Balthasar provides the music and sings the songs. But to reduce any character to a mere plot device is to do Shakespeare an injustice for he will give even minor characters the opportunity to make a significant impression on the audience as recognisable human beings:

- **Antonio** may be a minor member of Leonato's household, but his extravagant blustering challenge of Claudio is both an important counterweight to the near-tragic atmosphere and touching evidence of loyalty to his brother and niece.
- **Margaret**'s irrepressible talk and often bawdy sense of fun is clearly established. She is a valued member of Hero's entourage and her fondness for clothes and dressing up (which Borachio so skilfully exploits) is also revealed in her lingering description of the Duchess of Milan's gown.
- When **Friar Francis** takes on the unenviable task of trying to avert tragedy, his words are reasoned and thoughtful, echoing the play's 'noting' motif. His efforts to 'look for greater birth' persuade Leonato his daughter is innocent and offer him hope for the future.
- **Borachio** drinks (*boracho* in Spanish means 'drunk'). He is a villain with some initiative, who devises the plot to slander Hero; yet he possesses remnants of conscience, for he admits everything to Don Pedro and insists Margaret was blameless (but not before sensibly blaming Don John for putting him up to the deception).
- **Balthasar**'s main function is to sing the keynote song 'Sigh no more, ladies' at one of the key turning points of the play, yet Shakespeare also gives him some brief dramatic substance. When Balthasar fishes for compliments before singing his song, he echoes the play's 'noting' motif ('Note this before my notes, / There's not a note of mine that's worth the noting').

In Shakespeare's time, playwrights and audiences were not so much concerned with psychological realism as with character types and their functions. They tended to regard characters as figures in a developing story, to be understood by how they formed part of that story, and by how far they conformed to certain well-known types and fulfilled certain traditional roles. Even the major characters in *Much Ado About Nothing*, therefore, resemble in some ways the stock figures of villains, heroes and heroines.

When you write about characters in *Much Ado About Nothing*, you should therefore try to achieve a balance between analysing their personality, identifying the dramatic functions they fulfil and the dilemmas they face, and placing them in their social, critical and dramatic contexts. That style of writing is found all through this Guide, and that, together with the following brief discussions of four pairs of characters, can help your own written responses.

Two clowns

Dogberry and Verges are very much a comic double act. Their dramatic function is to discover the plot against Hero yet be so incompetent that the news is almost never reported to Leonato. The comic relief they bring also helps to balance the near-tragic events that surround them.

Dogberry was first played by Will Kemp, the company's resident comedian, who relied for laughs on his clowning, grimaces and extempore wit. Dogberry attempts to ape the elegant language of his superiors and fails conspicuously. But he is not merely a comic mangler of words. He has a range of moods: respectful to Leonato, condescending towards his partner Verges, outraged at the two captured villains. He is long-winded, smugly certain of his own worth and therefore absurdly incredulous that Conrade should presume to call him an ass. There is a laughable yet touchingly innocent dignity in his tirade against Conrade.

The function of Verges is to be the straight man in the comic double act and he has often been played as a small, ancient man in contrast to the more robust Dogberry. He is eager to assist and agree with his superior, who promptly puts him down whenever he shows the slightest hint of initiative.

Two royal brothers

Don John is from the start a brooding threatening presence, virtually silent amidst elegant talkers. An Elizabethan audience would automatically know that, as the illegitimate brother of Don Pedro, he was the play's villain (see page 70). Shakespeare uses an early scene with Don John and his two henchmen to establish him as an egocentric, misanthropic malcontent who envies other people's happiness and looks to cause trouble where he can.

Compared to some of Shakespeare's other villains, he is a rather stereotyped figure, not as threateningly dangerous, for example, as Iago in *Othello*, whom he resembles in the way he exploits the sexual hang-ups of his victims out of what Coleridge calls 'motiveless malignancy'. He is, in fact, too slow on the uptake to be a serious villain, for Borachio has to work hard to make him understand his plan.

Once the crisis has been provoked at the wedding, Shakespeare allows Don John to fade from the scene. The comedy allows no part in the final reconciliation for such an outcast. His flight from Messina and subsequent capture is only briefly reported so as not to spoil the celebrations.

Don Pedro is a Spanish prince and ruler of Sicily. He is assured and confident at the start of the play, an honoured guest in Leonato's house. During the recent military campaign he has apparently taken Claudio under his wing and continues to do so, now tutoring him in the art of courtship rather than war. The friendship forged in war between himself, Claudio and Benedick seems genuine, with the prince in the role of 'senior company officer'.

Like his brother, Don Pedro enjoys plotting and the sense of power and control it brings, although his deceptions are not maliciously intended. Both main plots are initiated by him and at first go exactly as he plans, until he is himself deceived, along with Claudio. The speed with which he sees an affront to his own honour, plus the support he gives to the public shaming of Hero, reveal a less attractive side to this elegant aristocrat. From this point on, he progressively loses control of events.

His remorse when the truth is revealed may be truly felt, yet it is not long before he and Claudio are again directing cuckold jokes at Benedick. By the end of the play he is a virtually silent observer of events who cuts a rather sad and lonely figure.

Two courtly lovers

Beatrice and Benedick may dominate the play but the main plot concerns Hero and Claudio, for it is their story which begins the action and drives all subsequent events. They are a very conventional young couple who happily conform to accepted rituals of aristocratic Elizabethan courtship and marriage – wooing by proxy, settlement of the dowry, formal betrothal and marriage ceremony. They seem clearly intended to contrast with the more individual and unconventional Beatrice and Benedick.

Hero is the typical dutiful and compliant young Elizabethan woman. She is informed that Don Pedro might woo her and given instructions on how to behave, only to discover that it is Claudio who wishes to marry her, a man in whom she has appeared to show no interest. Her name derives from the ancient Greek story of Hero and Leander and symbolises faithful love. Although largely silent and passive in the play in the presence of men, Shakespeare does give depth to her character in two intimate all-female scenes, where she shows sparks of imagination, envy and irritation (see pages 29–30 and 35). Even so, many modern actresses have found it hard to stomach her passivity and forgiveness in the face of Claudio's very public rejection.

Claudio is very much the model Elizabethan lord, courageous in battle and a close friend of the prince. But his youth and inexperience, combined with a distrust of women and a prickly sense of his own honour, leave him vulnerable to the machinations of Don John. While Elizabethan audiences may have seen nothing mercenary in Claudio's inquiring after Hero's inheritance and would also have understood his concern at being foisted with an unchaste bride, modern audiences often find him shallow and insensitive. Most unforgivable to modern minds is the public way he takes his revenge and his indifference to the news of Hero's death. His final contribution to the play is a singularly crass joke that Benedick is bound to be unfaithful to Beatrice.

Two scorners of love

The persistent 'doubleness' of the play is clearly seen in the closeness with which the Beatrice–Benedick plot both parallels and contrasts with the main plot. In the crucial church scene, for example, Shakespeare first brings the Hero–Claudio story to its crisis, which provokes the crisis in Beatrice and Benedick's relationship that results in Benedick's challenge of Claudio.

Beatrice and Benedick are without doubt the most memorable, complex and individual characters in the play and their journey from hostility to love is long and difficult. Despite their bristlingly witty encounters, it is obvious the two are mutually attracted. The play hints at earlier wounding encounters and even a previous unhappy romance (Act 2 Scene 1, lines 211–13), as if to suggest that their present antagonism is a protective shield against any repetition of earlier disappointments.

Their honest and courageous reaction to Hero's rejection is the moral centre of the play. Beatrice believes in her heart that her cousin is innocent and Benedick acts because he believes in his heart that she speaks the truth. Shakespeare, however, does not suggest that such a mutual respect and understanding is easy to achieve. To the very end there remain vestiges of their earlier suspicion and reluctance to commit.

Confirmed bachelor

Benedick talks from the start as if he were a 'professed tyrant' to women, but it is clearly a pose, as he himself almost admits (Act 1 Scene 1, lines 122–4). His friends' deception, together with his trust in Beatrice, leads him to a new maturity and a rejection of his old comfortable male comradeship.

He is paradoxically both serious and comic. If he is usually bested in word battles with Beatrice and mocked for his lovesick appearance, his response to Beatrice's command to 'Kill Claudio' is wholly admirable, and his resignation from the prince's service is spoken with manly dignity. Perhaps his most redeeming feature is his self-awareness, for he is almost always able to laugh at himself. Even when he is finally forced to recant his earlier stance against marriage, he does it so wholeheartedly that he turns mockery into respect. His final acknowledgement of his earlier foolishness could almost sum up the whole play: 'for man is a giddy thing, and this is my conclusion'.

Disdainful lady

Beatrice makes it clear from the start that she neither wants nor needs a husband, claiming she would rather hear her dog bark at a crow than a man swear he loved her, a statement clearly contradicted by her first words in the play – an enquiry about Benedick. She has the sharpest of barbed wits from which even Benedick is obliged to retreat, and is clearly a match for any man in the play. Like Shakespeare's other comic heroines, she has an independent spirit and a willingness to question the received wisdoms of the male hierarchy.

Shakespeare hints, too, at a softer, more vulnerable side to her nature. Born under a dancing star, she 'hath often dreamed of unhappiness, and waked herself with laughing'. Tricked into believing Benedick loves her, she likewise unhesitatingly renounces her former 'pride and scorn' and vows to give herself to him in marriage.

Beatrice is perhaps the most clear-sighted character in the play, never doubting Hero's innocence for a moment and seeing through Claudio's posturing ('Count Comfect, a sweet gallant surely'). She would eat Claudio's heart if she could, but even this formidable lady is forced to concede that she lives in a man's world where vengeance 'is a man's office'. Modern critics speculate on the meaning of her final silence: some see it as a willing acceptance of marriage, others doubt whether a free spirit like hers could ever accept such a subordinate role.

Perhaps Shakespeare provides a clue in the names. Beatrice comes from the Latin *beatrix*, meaning 'she who blesses'; Benedick comes from the Latin *benedictus*, meaning 'blessed'.

A note on examiners

Examiners do not try to trap or trick you. They set questions and select passages for comment intended to help you write your own informed personal response to the play. They expect your answer to display a sound knowledge and understanding of the play, and to be well structured. They want you to develop an argument, using evidence from the text to support your interpretations and judgements. Examiners know there is never one 'right answer' to a question, but always opportunities to explore different approaches and interpretations. As such, they welcome answers which directly address the question set, but which show origin-ality, insight and awareness of complexity. Above all, they reward responses which show your awareness that *Much Ado About Nothing* is a play for performance and which demonstrate that you can identify how Shakespeare achieves his dramatic effects.

Resources

Books

Harry L Berger, 'Against the Sink-a-Pace: Sexual and Family Politics in *Much Ado About Nothing*', in Marion Wynn-Davies (ed.), *New Casebooks: Much Ado About Nothing and The Taming of the Shrew*, Palgrave Press, 2001
An analysis of how the 'Messina Men's Club' creates male identity and how the play's concept of marriage is more complex than its happy ending might suggest.

Ralph Berry, *Shakespeare's Comedies: Explorations in Form*, Princeton University Press, 1972
Contains a thought-provoking chapter on 'Problems of Knowing' in *Much Ado About Nothing*.

Ralph Berry, *Shakespeare and Social Class*, Humanities Press Inc., 1988
Contains a discussion on relationships of rank in *Much Ado About Nothing*.

John Russell Brown (ed.), *Much Ado About Nothing and As You Like It: A Casebook*, Macmillan, 1979
A valuable selection of criticism up to the 1970s (including articles by Barbara Everett and Sherman Hawkins noted in this booklist).

S P Cerasano, 'Half-a-Dozen Dangerous Words', in Marion Wynn-Davies (ed.), *New Casebooks: Much Ado About Nothing and The Taming of the Shrew*, Palgrave Press, 2001
An historical study which shows the vulnerability of Elizabethan women to verbal attacks.

H B Charlton, *Shakespearian Comedy*, Methuen, 1938
Charlton sees comic heroines as the centre of the comedies' 'charm'. He argues that Shakespeare in his comedies gave his audience what they wanted: tales of romance and romantic courtship.

Linda Cookson and Bryan Loughrey (eds.), *Critical Essays on Much Ado About Nothing*, Longman Literature Guides, Longman, 1989
A wide ranging collection of essays aimed at a student audience, with useful 'afterthoughts' at the end of each essay to promote further thinking about the play.

John F Cox (ed.), *Shakespeare in Production: Much Ado About Nothing*, Cambridge University Press, 1997
A valuable edition which focuses on performance history and changing interpretations and is especially good on changing concepts of womanhood.

Juliet Dusinberre, *Shakespeare and the Nature of Women*, Macmillan, 1975
Argues that both Shakespeare's drama and elements of late Elizabethan society were feminist in sympathy.

Barbara Everett, '*Much Ado About Nothing*: Something of Great Constancy', 1961, in John Russell Brown (ed.), *Much Ado About Nothing and As You Like It: A Casebook*, Macmillan, 1979
A carefully argued article that sees the play as a clash of male and female worlds, with female humane values as the saving grace of the male Messina.

Barbara Everett, '*Much Ado About Nothing*: The Unsociable Comedy', in Marion Wynn-Davies (ed.), *New Casebooks: Much Ado About Nothing and The Taming of the Shrew*, Palgrave Press, 2001
Combines new critical approaches with perceptive insight into the play's concern with the interdependence of happiness and sorrow.

Penny Gay, *As She Likes It: Shakespeare's Unruly Women*, Routledge, 1994
A feminist account of the way productions of Shakespeare's comedies have altered over the last 50 years (an extract is reprinted in Marion Wynn-Davies, 2001 – see below).

Sherman Hawkins, 'The Two Worlds of Shakespearian Comedy', in John Russell Brown (ed.), *Much Ado About Nothing and As You Like It: A Casebook*, Macmillan, 1979
Examines the underlying patterns in *Much Ado About Nothing* and other comedies.

Jean E Howard, 'Antitheatricality Staged: The Workings of Ideology in Shakespeare's *Much Ado About Nothing*', in Marion Wynn-Davies (ed.), *New Casebooks: Much Ado About Nothing and The Taming of the Shrew*, Palgrave Press, 2001
Argues that a play does not passively reflect its society, but alters actively the way people think, through its plural and contradictory meanings.

Alexander Leggatt, *Shakespeare's Comedy of Love*, Methuen, 1974
Contains a very helpful chapter on *Much Ado About Nothing*.

Pamela Mason, *Much Ado About Nothing: Text and Performance*, Macmillan, 1992
A very readable text that includes detailed examination of several scenes, together with an account of a number of different productions.

J R Mulryne, *Shakespeare: Much Ado About Nothing*, Edward Arnold, 1965
Examines aspects of the play which critics have found problematic. Argues that in performance most of these 'problems' are resolved.

Carol Thomas Neely, *Broken Nuptials: Much Ado About Nothing*, Yale University Press, 1985 (an extract is in Gary Waller (ed.), *Shakespeare's Comedies*, Longman Critical Readers, Longman Press, 1991)
Argues that the play's 'broken nuptials' underline the women's reluctance to marry and the need for reformation of the men before a harmonious ending can be achieved.

Ruth Nevo, *Comic Transformations in Shakespeare*, Methuen, 1980
A chapter on *Much Ado About Nothing* examines how the Hero–Claudio main plot is challenged and almost 'inverted' by the Beatrice–Benedick sub-plot.

A P Rossiter, *Angel with Horns*, Longman, 1961
An essay on *Much Ado About Nothing* explores the play's concern with deception. It is also particularly good on Dogberry.

Roger Sales, *Much Ado About Nothing*, Penguin Critical Studies, Penguin Press, 1987
A useful introduction to the play and its sources, with analyses of three paired characters: Don John and Dogberry, Hero and Claudio, Beatrice and Benedick.

Brian Vickers, *The Artistry of Shakespeare's Prose*, Methuen, 1968
A valuable analysis of the structure and use of prose in Shakespeare's plays. The chapter on *Much Ado About Nothing* contains detailed examples from the play.

Marilyn L Williamson, *The Patriarchy of Shakespeare's Comedies*, Wayne State University Press, Detroit, 1986
A study of the power relationships in Shakespeare's comedies, particularly within marriage and the family.

Marion Wynn-Davies (ed.), *New Casebooks: Much Ado About Nothing and The Taming of the Shrew*, Palgrave Press, 2001
A stimulating selection of recent criticism (contains articles by Harry Berger, S P Cerasano, Barbara Everett, Penny Gay and Jean Howard noted in this booklist).

Films and audio books

Despite being a popular choice for the stage, there are relatively few film or TV versions of *Much Ado About Nothing*. A Hollywood silent film adaptation was made in 1926, two Russian film versions in 1956 and 1973, an American TV production in 1958 and an East German film in 1963, but it is unlikely that any of these are currently available.

The following versions are the most recent and most accessible:

BBC/Time-Life production (1984) with Robert Lindsay as Benedick and Cherie Lunghi as Beatrice. This has been judged a rather static and heavy-footed production, but it gives a clear traditional-style account of plot development and character.

Kenneth Branagh's film (1993) with Branagh as Benedick and Emma Thompson as Beatrice. A lively and highly watchable production which exploits the visual possibilities of film to the full. It has been described as a 'sure and intelligent translation of Shakespeare's comic energies into film rhythms and images'.

Four major versions are available on audio books in the series by Naxos, Harper Collins, Arkangel and BBC Radio Collection.

Much Ado About Nothing on the Web

If you type 'Much Ado About Nothing Shakespeare' into your search engine, it may find over 60,000 items. Because websites are of wildly varying quality, rapidly disappear or are created, no recommendation can safely be made. But if you have time to browse, you may find much of interest.